SELLING YOUR
CONFIDENCE

Forging A Successful Sales Career
From Mint Cookies To Martinis

JEAN WRIGHT

INDIE BOOKS
INTERNATIONAL

Girl Scouts® is a registered trademark of Girl Scouts of the United States of America (The use of Girl Scouts and its cookies is not an endorsement or sponsorship of this book.)
Girl Scout Cookies® is a registered trademark of Girl Scouts of the United States of America
Thin Mints® is a registered trademark of Girl Scouts of the United States of America
Do-si-dos® is a registered trademark of Girl Scouts of the United States of America
Tagalongs® is a registered trademark of Girl Scouts of the United States of America
The Pampered Chef® is a registered trademark of Pampered Chef, Ltd.
Jell-O® is a registered trademark of Postum Company, Incorporated
Kelly Girl® is a registered trademark of Kelly Properties, LLC
Wiffle® is a registered trademark of The Wiffle Ball, Inc.
Avon® is a registered trademark of Avon Products, Inc.
Tupperware® is a registered trademark of Dart Industries, Inc.
Disney® is a registered trademark of Disney Enterprises, Inc.
Mickey Mouse® is a registered trademark of Disney Enterprises, Inc.
Minnie Mouse® is a registered trademark of Disney Enterprises, Inc.
Tiffany & Co.® is a registered trademark of Tiffany and Company
Toastmasters® is a registered trademark of Toastmasters International

ISBN 13: 978-1-957651-33-0
Library of Congress Control Number: 2023902841

Author photo by Empire Photography
Cover designed by Steve Plummer Design
Interior designed by Amit Dey

INDIE BOOKS INTERNATIONAL®, INC.
2511 WOODLANDS WAY
OCEANSIDE, CA 92054
www.indiebooksintl.com

For Bernadette, Carolyn, and Luanne, the strong women who have inspired me with their confidence as a mother, daughter, and sister. And to Carol, my writing coach and cheerleader, for giving me the confidence I needed to write this book.

CONTENTS

—————•·————

PREFACE

I knew something wasn't quite right when I asked a group of entrepreneurs at a women's business group meeting whether they considered themselves salespeople. Of the fifty or so in attendance, about five brave souls raised their hands. As a longtime member of this organization, I knew there were more saleswomen in the audience who were holding back. I heard the phrase "sleazy used-car salesman" murmured in the crowd.

It was obvious the job title didn't sit well with them. As we explored their reluctance, many confessed they didn't want to be seen as aggressive. And only a few thought of their work, which almost always involved selling products or services, as sales. It wasn't until I started telling stories about why I loved being a sales professional that these ambitious women perked up and started seeing the potential of increasing their effectiveness without sacrificing their ethics.

This conversation with successful female entrepreneurs confirmed my suspicion that stereotypes about aggressive sales practices made many women in business uncomfortable. I knew that sales could be positive, even empowering, for both seller and buyer. But many in my audience had a hard time with the term and all the baggage that came with it.

Did they feel inferior about being salespeople? Did their limited understanding of sales also limit their business success? How could I help them see sales as more than self-interested greed? I knew at that moment: they needed some guidance to build confidence and authenticity as sales professionals.

Let's face it—we're all selling something. Sometimes we don't even realize it. Whatever the product or service we're sharing, we need to be viewed as capable and knowledgeable. Even better, we can be genuinely excited about the work we've chosen. Confidence in sales builds successful sales relationships as we become skilled experts who love what we're selling.

I never thought about being a salesperson as a profession until I just started doing it. I've sold just about everything in my sales career—office space, personnel services, kitchen products, and television and magazine ads, to name a few—lots of different products using basically the same sales techniques.

What I found is that selling is not about being aggressive or shifty like a used-car scammer. It's all about having confidence in your *ability* to make connections with your customer and sell well. In my presentations and mentoring, I've learned over and over that the old stereotypes are still strong. Convincing women entrepreneurs to own their role as sales professionals requires sharing actual life experiences I gained in my sales jobs. This book does just that, step-by-step outlining confidence-building practices, while sharing the experiences that shaped my lifelong career in sales.

WHAT'S NEW ABOUT THIS BOOK?

Most how-to-sell books promise to teach "proven" sales techniques to improve performance or guarantee higher commissions if you follow a certain formula. They generally teach approaches that fit the aggressive, masculine stereotypes that turn women and many men away from sales careers. These boilerplate strategies can't work for everyone, in every setting, with every customer. Even if they claim to be supported by the latest theories about persuasion or innovation or corporate excellence, these books need a lot of translation into your personal sales style and your actual product or service.

What new and experienced sales professionals need aren't formulaic strategies or interesting theories they have to translate into action. No matter how engaging these how-to-sell books can be, salespeople navigating the challenges of real-world situations need real-world insights to help them understand how to succeed in real-world sales.

I asked myself, "what are the stories none of these high-powered sales prescriptions share?" Formulas don't build confidence as we face the daily challenges of successful sales like: the miles you put on your feet and car when cold-calling, the feelings you have when doors are shut in your face, the loneliness of dealing with unexpected life events while maintaining the stamina to meet your goals, and the nagging (and self-sabotaging) worry that you are coming across as aggressive instead of showing who you really are—a confident sales professional.

How do we gain the confidence to keep going and get to the good stuff? Those are things like the surprise connection that opens up a whole new market, the customer relationships that last so long they become colleagues and friends, the big *yes* after a long day of cold-calling, the follow-up call that opens a door no one else in your firm could unlock, and the satisfaction of coming home to celebrate meeting quarterly goals and earning a solid bonus that helps your family weather hard times.

Building confidence comes from experience, and my own stories about those experiences are what makes this book stand out from all the others. I learned to be confident selling in the trenches.

I had little formal training when I started, but because someone saw potential in me, I grabbed the chance, and I learned what worked for me.

Would it have been easier if I had known what I was getting into? Maybe, but then I wouldn't have such great stories to tell— like being caught on a security camera while cold-calling in an office building, pitching closed-captioning to a famous Hollywood television producer, or stepping around horse manure while entertaining gamblers as the group sales director at a racetrack. I did say trenches. Those experiences and many others were confidence builders.

Whether I was selling products or services, I learned to overcome challenging situations. In this book I'll share tips on how to balance a career when dealing with economic and personal change, and how to be taken seriously as a woman who is confident in her role. It's my hope that I can help other salespeople face similar challenges more easily and build their successes as they build their sales careers.

I've written this book primarily for women, but I believe men can benefit from its lessons as well. Anybody wanting a satisfying sales career will find most of these insights useful. It's not just women who resist identifying with the stereotype of the sleazy used-car salesmen. (In fact, most car salespeople hate that stereotype, too.) Men don't have to fall into the traditional stereotypes and need to build self-confidence as much as women do. In my experience, many of my sales peers, both men and women, excelled because they built their own personal style of selling. They built successful careers by being authentic.

The real world is calling all of us to improve our sales abilities, because the workplace is evolving and changing. In today's post-pandemic world, more people than ever are changing careers.

Many will choose jobs they didn't think they would ever try. Some will start their own businesses or build a side business designing and selling a new product or service to meet new demands. Or an employer may add sales to an employee's job description, expecting them to shift roles without much training. With the right set of expectations and support, a new salesperson can sell just about anything and be very successful.

Whether we're pushed into sales or choose the profession, we can't succeed without the confidence to learn. I hope what you'll discover in this book will inspire you to think of sales as an adventure that you can take on with assurance. The highs and lows, the challenges, and the triumphs will become your greatest inspiration. For anyone exploring this career—looking for a job change, graduating from college, or seeking a fresh approach as an experienced salesperson—I know you can be successful, because confident sales come from qualities you already have: a desire to be authentic, a passion for your product or service, and the motivation to learn.

Jean Wright

1

GIRL POWER AND COOKIES

———•———

"**I**'m Thumbody!" I cradled the pint-sized embossed glass with pride.

It was the first validation of my sales success—a thumb-printed yellow smiley face on my incentive mug for selling Girl Scout treats. I was eleven, but to this day I still remember the joy I felt, holding my prize for going door-to-door selling cookies.

It was my first selling experience. Little did I know then I'd started a lifelong sales career with boxes of scrumptious confections and this tacky little mug as a reward. Over the years, those "branded" Girl Scout Cookies brought joy to my neighbors anticipating their annual arrival. There was a need—an insatiable need—for these cookie lovers to obtain mass quantities of their favorites and I was not going to let them down.

I learned how to meet this need in a sea of green-uniformed ten-to-twelve-year-olds, sitting at folding cafeteria tables in a beer-stained, stale-smelling fire hall basement in a Pittsburgh suburb. I didn't know it at the time, but this was my first sales meeting.

I felt inspired by our leader moms. "We get a lot of funds from our cookie sale so the troop can do fun things," I was told. *Oh boy,*

I thought, *we can go camping in the rain, make corny crafts for our parents, and go on field trips to planetariums.* It seemed worth it to me at the time.

We were given our goals: "Girls, sell at least fifty boxes if you want to be eligible for the prizes." So, I did the math and figured if I went to every house on my street and each neighbor bought at least one box, I would be halfway to my goal. Then I would venture out to the unexplored parts of my suburban neighborhood and sell the rest.

I felt optimistic about my success, although I had never sold anything in my young life. We were told to present ourselves as responsible young ladies while knocking on doors to ask for support of Troop 899's cookie sale. I had my marching orders, including the all-important money collection envelope and the permission slip for my parents to sign. I was ready to hit the streets. Or so I thought.

But my parents didn't get it. I handed them the permission slip, which they promptly handed back to me, unsigned. "No one from this house is going door-to-door to ask for money," my dad said.

My mother agreed: "We'll just give you a check."

My parents were embarrassed that the neighbors would think *their* child was pressuring them to buy something they might not want. Salespeople they were not. My dad grew up in Europe, so maybe he didn't understand the fundraising requirement for members of an organization like Girl Scouts. And they had bought into the sleazy sales stereotype without a second thought.

I convinced them both that I was asking people to donate to a good cause, and every customer received delicious cookies in return. Didn't they know that for the amazing price of seventy-five cents a box (they're five dollars now), I was fulfilling my customers' desire to have unlimited quantities of Tagalongs and Do-si-dos? It was the only time of year one could easily justify eating an entire box of Thin Mints in record time (usually alone, in a place where you don't have to share).

One by one, I addressed my parents' objections—the first hurdle in the sales process—and they signed the permission slip. My sales career was about to begin.

If they only knew how many streets away from our house I would walk to persuade people, mostly strangers, to buy as many boxes as possible. I would finish one street and then push myself to go the distance to the next. Who cared if it was getting close to dinnertime, or the streetlights were coming on? I had cookies to sell.

Walking along a new road in my uniform, as the next row of houses appeared I was confident they were mine to conquer, with no other Girl Scout selling cookies in sight. More streets, more houses, more customers, and more money.

I simply knocked on doors, inviting my future customers to take advantage of a limited offer, "Order your cookies now before they are sold out! How many boxes would you like?"

I don't think Girl Scout Cookies ever really sold out, but I wanted a decision on the spot. There was no time to delay— urgency was the key. I closed sweet deal after sweet deal. When I came home with a bulging envelope, my parents were impressed with my success.

I do not remember winning any major awards for top seller, or even what the big prizes were. If there was an award ceremony, I wasn't there. But I loved my "I'm Thumbody!" mug, the prize for selling fifty boxes. I was also proud I'd met my own goal, persuading people to buy something they needed and wanted from me. Of course, the product sold itself, but it had some extra help from a smiling blond girl with a green sash and beanie.

Decades later, my mother, now in her nineties, fessed up with something startling to me, a bit of regret in her voice, "I can't believe

I almost thwarted you from selling those cookies." She had carried some guilt all these years as she watched me succeed in my sales career—as group sales director at a racetrack, marketing rep and sales manager for two personnel companies, account executive for a magazine and television station, membership recruiter for a chamber of commerce, marketing rep selling closed-captioning services, and general sales manager for a global office rental company. She is truly proud of me now and regretted her impulse to hold me back from what she calls my "God-given talent" for sales.

Even today, I appreciate the valuable skills I learned in Girl Scouts about selling. Where else can you get free training? We were taught how to cold-call, present the product, and close the deal. Of course, I did not know these were sales techniques. I was just following instructions.

I wonder how many women in sales, former Girl Scouts, now realize the cookie drive was the start of their sales careers. Fifty, seventy-five, one hundred cookie boxes sold and flash forward twenty years to closing high-powered sales deals.

My cookie-selling experiences made me feel more confident about my communication skills. I did not need the help of anyone else to sell successfully. I could convince people to part with their money, to buy something they wanted, and, in fact, could not resist. Plus, using an effective sales tool, the art of persuasion, I also sold my parents on the idea to let me do it. After that hard sell, I had no problem knocking on strangers' doors and asking them to buy. I loved the thrill of the hunt. Cookie lovers: I'm coming for you.

I also felt motivated by social values. I not only met my personal goals, but I also worked as a team member for the common good. It never occurred to me that as a girl I had anything to overcome. I wore my iconic green uniform that represented my company. I was a valuable member of an organization that was bigger than me.

That's why I kept the "I'm Thumbody!" mug, a reminder of what inspired me to sell all those years ago and what continues to inspire me today. As I continued my sales adventure, all I had to do was follow those cookie crumbs of knowledge along the trail to my success.

2

PRESENTING THE PACKAGE

My career has taught me that everything we do in life involves marketing. From the moment we step outside our front door, we are a package, presenting ourselves to the world, from what we wear to what we say. What we do with the package we create will determine our success.

Dressing professionally makes a first impression even before you say a word. The type of business we represent determines the dress code. If you're getting back into the workforce after being home with the kids, be up to date with fashion trends and don't wear that favorite jacket you saved from the mid-2000s. Look like you live in current times. Even if you are on a virtual call, professional attire is still important, at least from the waist up.

But a first impression isn't just about your dress code. Your confidence sells the customer on working with you. I've been in a room where a woman or man stands up in smart, professional attire but then introduces themselves and their business with little eye contact and in a subdued voice. What a disappointment.

If you want to sell your product, look the part and tell the room about it, as if you were talking excitedly to your best friend. It's apparent when someone doesn't believe in their own personal or business value when they speak quietly and fail to make eye contact with their audience. You won't build a connection if you're not selling yourself. If you're not selling yourself, then you're not showing confidence in what you have to offer.

This is also the moment when you build trust. I naturally trust people who make eye contact with me when we're talking, or just when they're presenting to a group. When someone introduces themself, selling their entire package, they build trust when they help me see their confidence, excitement, and purpose. That's how a relationship is built. A business deal will follow.

How can we be more confident when presenting ourselves as a package? First, we need to be aware of the things that make us feel self-conscious and shift our performance to overcome those old ideas. When I was growing up, I felt self-conscious about my height. In school, I was always in the last row with the tallest boy for class pictures. I often sat in the back of the classroom because I feared no one could see over my head. I should have felt confident about myself as someone who stood out, but I didn't feel worthy of that attention.

I had to learn that my total package included not only my height but a tall personality to go with it. It took time for me to feel comfortable and learn how to make an entrance. I eventually figured out how to present myself, so I was remembered for who I was and not just because I towered over the crowd.

Eventually I learned that being tall helped me command a room. I began to feel more comfortable speaking in front of people. When you're the center of attention, you better have something memorable to say, and use every tool at hand to keep their eyes on you. If you're not prepared, or if you're distracted by self-consciousness, your audience will lose confidence in you, and you may lose that connection and its sale potential. As a result, you'll wear away at your own confidence.

I knew I needed to be prepared to deliver a strong package with every introduction or presentation. To ensure I had my act together, I joined Toastmasters, an international organization that teaches public-speaking skills. I was confident in my ability to talk in front of an audience, but I wasn't sure I was doing it correctly. I found a local chapter and delivered speeches at their monthly 7:30 a.m. meetings. Being "on" at that hour of the morning was a challenge. Memorizing and making speeches involved a lot of practice and multiple mugs of caffeine.

My goal was to speak in a professional manner without a script but trying to memorize my notes really tested my confidence. If I didn't rehearse enough, I lost my way and started scrambling for words. I learned to gather my inner strength and confidently finish my speech, no matter what.

After we delivered our speeches, other members critiqued our efforts, helping us hone our speaking skills. We learned how to use voice inflection, create visual pictures, inject humor, use natural gestures, and tell stories. These basic but vital persuasive techniques kept the audience glued to a speaker's every word. They became an essential part of my package.

In many situations, you don't even realize how a strong self-presentation can affect someone else. I served as president of our community's social organization and a new resident had been skeptical about joining. Our development is in a rural area—completely opposite from the suburban Philadelphia neighborhood this woman had moved from. She told me a story about her husband, who, while showing her around our town, drove past the farm and feed store. She said she broke down in tears fearing they had moved to Green Acres.

After attending the meeting and hearing my presentation about our organization, she confessed that because I was professionally dressed and spoke well, she knew that she would feel comfortable with our group. I represented a community she could fit into, not that different from her previous neighborhood. I presented a package that she could relate to and sold her on joining our club. To this day, she talks about the impact of her first impression of me as anything but Green Acres; the result was that her membership provided her with lifelong friends and a strong community.

Other women I've known have used their attitude and image as confidence builders. A business coach told me that wearing high heels makes her feel empowered when she delivers her message to an audience. It was amazing to learn that something as simple as how she *felt* in those shoes built her confidence. It's not just what you wear, though—it's how you prepare. One female CEO confessed to me that she sings a rock anthem in her car before addressing a crowd or going into a meeting. It is her way of gathering energy and assurance for presentations.

Over time, I've learned to arrive prepared and be myself when speaking to groups or joining a meeting so that my confidence stays strong. Then I have the audience in the palm of my hand. Voilà. I've sold the package. And that's what it's all about—being comfortable presenting yourself in a professional way, visually and verbally, bringing confidence to just about everything you do.

3

LEARNING TO "WALK THE LINE": RED FLAGS AND ME TOO

M y sales experiences started with me feeling "I'm Thumbody" special, but once I decided to pursue a sales career, I quickly learned that the joy of selling is just one part of the career journey.

With every new job, there is a learning curve. Each new opportunity means we need to figure out how to navigate the culture and new rules of our office and company. It's important not to make mistakes and recover as quickly as we can when we inevitably do cross a line invisible to a newbie. And what about those learning experiences that we remember forever because they were serious red flags we should not have ignored?

Over the years I've learned how to walk the line between professional and personal behavior. I was lucky in my early career days to have sidestepped minefields that could have landed me in trouble. Sometimes experiencing uncomfortable circumstances will teach you what to look out for in the future. Remember, once you recover, these red-flag encounters make great stories.

RED FLAG #1

Beware of a business owner who is looking for the "nice Catholic girls" (or some other nonprofessional, sexist, or odd category) to work for their business. Always ask to see the actual product you are selling and make sure it is *real*.

I was looking for part-time employment in high school when a classmate told me about her job as a telemarketer for a real estate newspaper. Her boss wanted to hire more high school girls, just like her, to work for him after school and on weekends.

Previously, I had worked as a prep cook at the Murphy Mart and disliked the work. I could never seem to please the lady manager who had a seriously bad attitude. Anyway, making Jell-O salads and frying breaded fish shapes were not skills I needed for a college application. I thought nothing could be worse than that. So, I applied to become a "telephone solicitor," as they called it, and got the office phone job.

I never aspired to be a telemarketer. Even back then, people outside the business thought of the work as annoying, persistent calls, always asking for money at ungodly times of the day. But it was sales and, like selling the cookies, I thought I might actually enjoy it.

What I didn't know was the difference between a legitimate business and a shady setup. We worked in an office in a mall complex, so it had a real address—legit, right? The setup was professional enough, too, desks with phones arranged like a classroom in front of a big whiteboard tallying *yeses* and *nos* from our solicitation calls for the day.

I called endless lists of people on evenings and weekends, anyone who owned real estate from Maine to Alaska, especially those with swampland in Florida, asking them to advertise their out-of-state property in our newspaper.

Soon I had become *that* telephone solicitor, the most annoying weekend caller. I felt bad when a Sunday morning contact kindly said, "I'm leaving for church now, honey, I can't talk now." And I couldn't blame the irritated person who snapped, "Don't you know this is Mother's Day? Could you call me another time?" What nerve I had, calling people on Sundays and holidays.

I also got a crash course on geography and city names. I talked to a lady in Decatur, Illinois, reviewing her address for accuracy, saying, "*Dec*-a-tour, correct?" Instantly she knew from my pronunciation that I was not from those parts. She sensed I was probably calling her from some legitimate newspaper business in far-flung Pennsylvania, which of course, I was. Except it wasn't legitimate at all.

It was a standard setup for telemarketing. We had a quota of calls to make and specific *yes* goals for the day. We spoke lines from a scripted message, and recited the same for each call to every unsuspecting landowner. I tried to learn how to properly deliver my script to the people I was calling, but most simply preferred to hang up on me. There was no training.

My job was to persuade them to say, "Yes, I'd like more information about selling my out-of-state property" and mail them advertising rates. After getting used to hearing *no*, it didn't take long for me to build some confidence and sound "nicer" to persuade my customers to say *yes*.

When the boss came in—we'll call him Joe, to protect the guilty—he expected a stack of envelopes ready to be mailed out to all the *yeses* we received that day. He was a middle-aged Italian man

with a strong personality. All of us teenage phone solicitors anticipated that daily "surprise" visit with dread.

Joe seemed like a nice guy at first but when the stack of envelopes addressed to his potential victims did not touch the ceiling, he
would explode with rage and accuse us of failure. Then the tantrum
began as he threw the envelopes on the floor, sputtering out of the
room mumbling what I assumed were four-letter words in Italian.
It could have been worse—at least he didn't throw the envelopes at
us. We just had to restack and count them all over again.

Joe's minion—we'll call him Bruce—sat in the back of the
room making follow-up calls. He looked like a nerdy accountant,
and sat behind us, never moving, as if chained to his chair, even eating his meals at his desk. We figured he was probably reporting back
to Joe if we were slacking off. Bruce made the follow-up calls from
the letters we sent and supposedly closed deals for the high-priced
ads. He was like a dog, obedient to his master who tossed him little
treats when he made a sale.

I left this job after my senior year to go to college, and soon
learned the real estate newspaper did not exist, and Bruce was closing deals that put money into his pocket and Joe's. The more people
he could swindle, the richer he would be. My parents called me at
school to share the news that Joe was convicted of fraud and sent
to jail. I'm not sure what happened to Bruce. My dad said he was
surprised I wasn't subpoenaed to appear as a witness in court.

What really angered me was the fact that Joe took advantage of
naive high school girls to do his dirty work. We wouldn't ask questions, accepted low hourly wages, and increased his profit margin
while earnestly trying to please him. I also felt bad for all those people I called like the property owner in *Dec*-a-tour, the real victims of
his fraudulent scheme. I swore that the next job I had would be with
a business that had ethical standards.

RED FLAG #2

Don't accept rides from your boss, whether you think he's been flirting with you or not. And remember, harassment is more than a nuisance. Report the jerk.

When I returned home during winter break, I looked for temporary work to earn extra spending money. The Kelly Girl agency sent me out on a unique assignment—to promote a new printing business in town. It was to be my first experience cold-calling in person.

I learned that just opening the front door and expecting people to sign up for huge, commission-earning orders doesn't happen overnight. Building a client base is one of the most important aspects of running a new business. Forty years ago, there was no social media to spread the word, just snail mail, phone calls, and knocking on prospects' doors. Nor was there social media with "New Store Open" messages flooding the cyber universe.

I was given well-produced flyers and branded tablets to distribute as I drove around to shops and office buildings. I remember enjoying the freedom of being in my car and meeting new people as I dropped off materials introducing the new local printing franchise.

The owner—we'll call him Fred—seemed very impressed with my hustle to bring in new clients. Business was starting to pick up and he always complimented me on my efforts. Then he started complimenting my appearance. Of course, I felt good about looking professional and being appreciated for the hard work I put into my workplace package. It never occurred to me that he was actually checking me out.

I used our family car for my daily marketing calls, and I enjoyed getting out of the office, especially when I suspected

Fred was starting to flirt with me. It was a first, while working, so I couldn't believe it was happening. For one thing, he was quite unattractive, and a married man with children. I was nineteen years old, which made his flirtation feel unnatural and strange, to me that is.

But I kept my distance and stayed out of the office as much as I could, until the fateful day my car had to go into the shop, so my mother dropped me off at work. I had some filing to do so I just sat at my desk making calls. When it was time to leave for the day, Fred offered to drive me home. I thoughtlessly accepted, thinking it would save my mother a trip to pick me up.

Quickly, the ride went south. Fred kept looking over at me, explaining that he wanted to "be" with me and that since he was having marital problems it would be okay. I looked at his unappealing, red-pocked middle-aged face with disbelief and dread. I especially didn't want him to try and kiss me, so I moved close to the door. I told him that not only was I not interested, but that he was being inappropriate.

The car couldn't get to my house fast enough. His hand was slowly reaching toward my knee. As we rounded the corner to my street, I jumped out as he pulled up to my house.

I didn't have the nerve to tell my mother or the temp service that my boss, ugly Fred, had propositioned me. I just wanted to forget it. Besides, I suspected the temp service probably wouldn't believe their client would do such a thing. I only had to work there a few more days before heading back to school, so I tried to be out of the office as much as possible, avoiding any further interaction.

Fred had a saying that went, "Sometimes someone will disappoint you in life." Well, that could not have been truer. Little did

I know this wasn't the last experience I'd have. Office harassment would replay itself in the not-too-distant future.

As I continued in college, majoring in radio and TV, I dreamed of being a famous journalist. Like most schools, mine didn't quite prepare me for the real *business* of the fourth estate, selling advertising. I don't remember ever hearing about sales jobs as a career when I was taking my radio and TV classes.

I interned at a local TV station to learn about the news business and to get the credits I needed to graduate so I could become the next Barbara Walters. I had a ride in the station's helicopter, went on location with a female reporter, and was propositioned by the male news director in the parking lot. Those were my most memorable moments at this place.

The news director followed me to my car when I was leaving one night and asked me for a date. I didn't even think he knew me, let alone would start stalking me in a dark parking lot. After saying *no*, I sped off feeling like that was all I was worth to him when I expected to be treated professionally. I felt extremely uncomfortable about returning there, but I had to finish my internship.

I was always afraid he'd repeat his invitation, this time not taking *no* for an answer. But I never told anyone about the inappropriate behavior of a man twice my age who was supposed to be mentoring a twenty-one-year-old college intern about the TV news business. When I saw his name years later as the news director at another station, those memories flooded back. It was then I understood how women feel now about reliving bad memories of their boss's unwanted advances. It's a sometimes frightening disappointment you never forget. I should have reported the jerk.

RED FLAG #3

Don't take a job just because someone else thinks you can do it. They may be desperate, wrong about your ability to do the work, or have an ulterior motive. But if you find yourself in a job you should have refused, hold your professional boundaries, prove to them you can do it better than they thought you would, and be ready to move on to a better opportunity.

After I graduated from college, my mother, who worked with a public relations professional with great local connections, found me a job with a better salary than the entry-level news writer radio work I was doing. Everyone said it would be a great adventure, and exactly what I needed. I decided to try my luck (literally) as a group sales director at a thoroughbred racetrack in West Virginia.

I had never been to the track, never gambled on horses, nor did I ever want to live in West Virginia. But when you're fresh out of college, you have to start somewhere. Besides, what is there to lose? That was the last time that old cliché would ring true to me.

I would say it was a one-horse town but that would not be accurate. There were a *lot* of elderly racehorses and very few traffic lights. I was told that what this racetrack needed were more gamblers who would eat, drink, and bet their mortgages on old horses. Management was desperate for someone to lure in fans and introduce them to racing. A recession was looming, and large group events would help keep the racetrack afloat. Someone enthusiastic, young, and charismatic, like me, would be perfect for the task.

The woman temporarily handling the position was the secretary to the public relations director—let's call him Mr. PR King. He was the track's flashy, high-maintenance, ego-driven marketer with a gold chain necklace adorning his hairy chest always visible through his open-collared shirt. His only job seemed to be entertaining big-stakes gamblers and out-of-town sports celebrities in the clubhouse lounge. The former group sales director had retired, and the secretary's job was to keep up with Mr. PR King.

Being the group sales director sounded attractive—emphasis on *director*. Wow, I had a title and a reserved parking space. Finally, I was "Thumbody!" Before this, I had never thought about taking a sales job after graduation. I suddenly considered it as a real career.

Let me first say, it wasn't as glamorous as I'd expected, and it was a lot of hard and lonely work. But I learned a lot—how to advertise and sell "A Night at the Races" package deals to bus companies and social groups. I met gamblers, horse trainers, and small-town people who, basically, weren't at all like me. I booked and hosted large groups at the racetrack, most of whom arrived on buses, like AARP groups and Moose Lodges.

They loved going to the Winner's Circle to get their picture taken with the sweaty horse that just made them twenty-five dollars richer. I was the promoter in high heels who gingerly stepped in the muddy manure next to the agitated winner with the track photographer. The senior citizens were usually tipsy—kissing the horse on the face for the photo if they had a winning bet.

"What's a nice girl like you doing in a place like this?" was the nicest compliment I received while working there. Most visitors to the racetrack seemed to think I was better than that place, which I was. They seemed concerned about me, and they probably should have been. That type of environment attracted some undesirable characters and bad behaviors. And predictably, it was the seedy setting that drove me away, thanks to the VP of marketing, my remote boss, who crossed the line.

After the races, the staff would enjoy socializing at the restaurant and hotel on the grounds. It was the only place in the entire town to enjoy a great meal, have a drink, and dance to a live band. I mean, the *only* place. I was in my early twenties and having fun after a long workday was always something to look forward to.

We were owned by a corporation, so the out-of-town executives visited periodically to check in on us. The VP would visit and meet with me to discuss sales strategies. He seemed very professional, and I respected him and his position. After our meetings, he and the other executives would treat us to dinner at the hotel restaurant.

One night after dinner, my boss praised my work while we had drinks at the hotel bar, and we discussed whether there would be future opportunities at the corporate level. I knew I wasn't going to stay in nowheresville for longer than I needed to. What I didn't know, as a young woman in the business world, was that asking for such a promotion could open the door to other "offers," which did not actually pertain to my job.

As we were saying good night, he leaned in. "Do you want to talk more about your future in my hotel room?" I had gained respect for him as a mentor, and it was at that moment that my entire view of him as a person changed—from a professional guy in a suit to a slimeball. I had thought he was taking me seriously.

I couldn't believe he turned out to be *that* type of guy. What a disappointment. I was not interested in discussing my future in his hotel room. I never reported this instance to anyone at the racetrack or to HR corporate. I was a lowly twenty-three-year-old racetrack employee in a small town in "West, by god, Virginia" and they wouldn't believe an accusation against the VP of marketing, would they?

I imagine that in a racetrack environment it was probably acceptable behavior for women to be hit on, no matter who was doing the hitting. But what makes this different is the behavior of a corporate executive preying on an employee twenty years younger. I did learn some lessons though.

LESSON LEARNED #1

Talk about your job status and future career plans only in professional settings.

LESSON LEARNED #2

Ask if your employer has harassment training and take it. This is a mandated course at most companies today. It's always best to find out to whom and how to report information about higher-ups who cross a line before it happens.

The printing store guy, the news director, and the VP all tried to prey on me—but I shut them down. It did build my confidence to know I could stand up for myself and do the right thing. That might have been the most important lesson of all these red flags. I learned how to walk the professional line and field bad behavior, but now I know I should have reported it or talked to someone.

Reporting harassing behavior just wasn't a "thing" you did back in the '70s and '80s—but it is now. Stand up for yourself. Use the HR supports you need to make your workplace healthy and safe.

4

BUILDING A SALES CAREER AND RELOCATING TO THE BIG CITY

———— • ————

"**I**t's not just a job; it's an adventure!" was a familiar slogan once used by Navy recruiting. In the military context, an adventure would usually involve risk or hazard—like jumping out of a plane, piloting a big battle cruiser, or fighting an enemy. In sales careers, relocation is probably the closest parallel: exciting, risky, and definitely an adventure.

In college, I took a physical education class called "Adventure and Experience." We learned to walk confidently on high two-line traverses between trees and rappelled from a cliff. I never dreamed I would do either of those things because I was afraid of heights. But I considered the class a worthy adventure because I appreciated the risky opportunities, and it was something I could feel good about accomplishing.

Throughout my career, I approached relocating for each job opportunity in the same way—as an adventure—learning a new skill, moving to a new place, and meeting new people. So, where's the best place for a job to offer more adventure and high-impact experience? A big city with innumerable opportunities.

Flash back to nowheresville, West Virginia, where I was motivated to move by a downturn in the economy that ended my job at about the time I was ready to go.

My sister, a recent college graduate, was seeking employment with a new congressman in Washington, DC, on Capitol Hill. She had helped on his campaign and had high hopes of being hired full-time. We packed the car and drove to the promised land in search of a new adventure for both of us.

RELOCATION RULE #1

Have a plan before you leave—and be prepared for surprises.

We needed a home base while job hunting, so we found inexpensive accommodations to fit our conservative budget and allowed ourselves one to three months to secure employment. Then, unexpected circumstances came into play. Don't they always?

Within a few days of settling into our rented room, a blizzard hit the city and totally halted our job-hunting plans. It only takes two or more inches of snow to affect daily life in DC and this was much bigger. Roads were impassible, power was iffy, and we got a little bored waiting for snowplows to dig us out.

So we made the best of it—creating snow angels in a grassy traffic circle that featured a statue of an imposing man, our local protector. We managed to get by with cheap sandwiches from the "gourmet" deli down the street, and microwaved ramen noodle dinners to save money. We were glad we had built in realistic expectations of living frugally for up to three months.

Then, just as the streets began to clear, my group sales director experience at the track got me in the door sooner than expected.

After a month of interviewing, I was offered a marketing rep position at a personnel agency.

The owner of this private firm said his first impression of me was that I dressed for success. That was quite a compliment since I had just wiped the traces of grimy racetrack mud off my high heels. Actually, I'd retailored myself with a stylish, conservative business suit perfect for DC. It was kind of like my Mary Tyler Moore moment—new city, new job, new outfit, and tossing my hat into the air with joy.

My sister finally got the Capitol Hill job with the new member of Congress, Tom Ridge, and before long I was recruited to play on their office softball team. (They must have been desperate for players.) I had little experience other than playing Wiffle ball as a kid, but I faked it as the pitcher and was pretty good. It was a thrill to throw softballs to congressmen and their staff members on the Ellipse with the White House in view. I was even invited to sit in on a session of Congress by Congressman Ridge who made us feel like VIPs. I kind of liked being around famous and influential people, something I enjoyed in my relocation adventure.

RELOCATION RULE #2

Know your worth *before* relocating and don't settle for anything less.

I beat the streets in DC for a couple years and brought in lots of business. Then I found that working for a personnel company had its benefits—one of my clients was hiring for a marketing rep position. Knowing my adventurous spirit and having no fear of stepping off that cliff, I applied and started new work in Washington.

This business was associated with the television industry and closed-captioning, so I was tasked with obtaining funds from advertisers and producers to underwrite this service for TV shows and home videos. The long-range plan for me included a move to their Hollywood office where all the action was, not to mention being around celebrities. Now the adventure was turning into relocation glamour with the allure of Tinseltown calling.

Hollywood, here I come. Or so I thought. LA was a world away and had a significantly higher cost of living than what I was used to. Even though I was told about the plan to relocate when hired, a salary increase for a move was never discussed in our negotiations. I had to step up quickly and confidently.

For about a year at the DC office, I had demonstrated my value by bringing in new business, but I still had to negotiate my salary to afford higher LA rent. I did my homework and presented these costs to my managers. I overheard them behind closed doors ranting about being blindsided by my "demands." Instead of backing down, I kept pushing. This was the first time I felt assertive about standing up for myself and I held my ground.

Knowing I was worth every penny made me patient and persistent. I finally got the cost-of-living increase. I had already proven I was valuable to the business, and they didn't want to lose me.

NEGOTIATION LESSON

Do the most important negotiations upfront when offered a job; it will save a lot of anxiety.

The blood, sweat, and determination were all worth it. Just like seeing the White House from the softball field in DC, the image of the iconic Hollywood sign as I walked through the studio lot to my office was surreal. Even when that dense gray-green LA smog obscured it, the sign never lost its legendary luster.

I regularly sighted actors and singers like Dolly Parton, Phil Collins, and Sylvester Stallone walking casually around the lot. Audience laughter from sitcoms and game shows permeated the air. Bumping into Tony Danza in the hallway on my way to lunch or standing in line at Fatburger behind that kid from *The Cosby Show* was a common experience. But nothing would top standing in the restroom line one night next to comedian Robin Williams after his hilarious stand-up routine at The Comedy Store on Sunset Boulevard. His sweaty cheeriness resulting from his energized performance was memorable.

One of my big clients was Aaron Spelling Productions. The producer even invited me for a visit to the set of *The Love Boat*. The sight of scantily clad actors with perfect bods prancing around the azure-blue painted soundstage, the backdrop for the cruise ship scenes, was so kitschy it was a real bonus.

I knew the right people at the networks, which allowed me exclusive access for tickets to *The Tonight Show* and just about any sitcom that had a live audience. I had meetings at the studio lot where the series *L.A. Law* was filmed and was introduced to my favorite actors from the show, including the dreamy Jimmy Smits.

My work friend Susan and I went out one night to celebrate her birthday at a Hollywood bar and Jimmy was there with some friends. He asked her to dance when she told him it was her birthday. Then, we talked to him about the show, and he couldn't have been nicer. Afterward, Susan and I kept saying how unbelievable that experience was. What was not to like about the excitement of being in Hollywood?

Back at *L.A. Law*, I was fortunate that my client Steven Bochco was a proponent of closed-captioning. The big TV producers knew the benefits of reaching hearing-impaired people by putting captions on their shows. They were doing good things for humanity and their ratings and that's what helped us sell the service.

RELOCATION RULE #3

Know the challenges of your new location. If you move to an area prone to natural disasters, be prepared to handle the inevitable.

The most life-changing moment during my time in LA offered a different kind of excitement. One morning, I woke up to a 5.9 magnitude earthquake after living there for ten months. The quake rocked my world. I watched everything around my shaking apartment being violently tossed from shelves and off walls. My car moved one foot over the line on the deck from where it was parked the night before. This was the Whittier Narrows quake, centered near downtown LA. (Little did I know that a few years later the Northridge quake would damage my apartment building so badly it would be condemned. Thank goodness I had moved before the really big one.)

I thought about dashing out of my apartment during the tumult. I looked out my door into the hallway expecting my neighbors would be running for their lives, but there was no movement. I realized then that I was totally unprepared for this natural disaster. My neighbors were most likely huddled in their bathrooms or standing inside a doorframe—procedures taught to Californians to prepare for these terrifying circumstances.

The aftershocks continued for the next week and kept unnerving me. My boyfriend, Tom, from Philadelphia, visited the following weekend. It was one-hundred degrees and there was still a lot of shaking going on. He had to experience it to believe it. We even called it "Shake 'N Bake weekend." Without question, it was time to move. We started considering how and when I could relocate back to the East Coast.

We had met years ago in college, but it was that month that we decided to finally get engaged. I loved my job, but I needed to be on solid ground, and I wanted to be with him back East. So, love (and fear of earthquakes) eventually sent me to Philadelphia a few months later. My appreciation for adventure was beckoning again but, in this case, it was purely for personal reasons.

The City of Brotherly Love and LA couldn't be more opposite. In fact, I moved out in February and my LA friends thought I was crazy moving east in the middle of winter. The fresh California produce I used to buy at Ralphs on Ventura Boulevard was replaced with plastic-wrapped wilting vegetables at a suburban Philadelphia ACME Market. Even with snow beneath my feet that winter, I was relieved the ground wasn't moving.

RELOCATION RULE #4

New city, need a job? Sign-up at a personnel agency for temp work—it may lead to permanent employment.

With no glamorous entertainment business in sight, I returned to a familiar line of work with another personnel agency, managing one of their suburban offices. I was also the sole outside sales rep tasked with cold-calling every business in the vicinity. Since I had experience building a client base in DC, I just followed my instincts and continued being successful in bringing in more clients with my cold-calling skills.

I found that relocation *can* be an adventure again, whatever the reason, and I continued to enjoy that feeling throughout my career. As we moved over the years, I learned more about how my decisions guided me into new paths.

In Philly, after all that personnel agency experience, it dawned on me that there was a reason these companies were so successful—they helped people find good jobs. What was I waiting for? Once again, I knew what I needed to do.

I finally learned that putting my money where my mouth was, so to speak, benefitted my job searches. Why not take advantage of the product I had been selling and be a customer? Most personnel agencies have temp-to-perm jobs, and I needed a permanent job to pay for the wedding. I found a placement that met that financial goal so my fiance and I could start a new adventure together.

This resource required confidence to manage—I had to do research, apply, and interview, and I put my best self out there many times before I found the right placement, which was a solid job but not a great adventure. And, of course, after we were married, we relocated once again, and I had to repeat the process. I was able to parlay my previous sales experience into a temp job, which led to a full-time sales assistant position with a global computer manufacturer. I was back to having the professional adventure that fueled my satisfaction in sales work.

I worked directly with the sales manager and supported his dynamic team of reps who sold to Fortune 100 accounts. I knew nothing about the tech world, so I leaned in and learned more, and became a computer expert. I really liked the work and my coworkers.

My boss considered me an important contributor to the group and not just an administrative assistant in the sales department. I was "Thumbody" again. We developed a great camaraderie that encouraged the whole team to be more successful—an important foundation for sales teams, whose success or failure shouldn't rest only on their top performers. Two-hour lunches were not uncommon, and soon, we all knew each other well.

There were a lot of men in the group. I had learned from previous experience how to set parameters for professional behavior and used that knowledge to build strong coworking relationships. Our team earned a lot of respect within the company with high sales numbers and customer satisfaction, something we could all be proud about.

Professionally, taking on a new adventure was like rappelling off that cliff in college. It felt scary to take that step into the abyss but having confidence from my past experiences and training advanced me to the next level to ultimately reach my goals—a better job, higher salary, and satisfaction with my work. Just allowing myself to hit a few rocks and bounce around a bit, I kept a steady grip on that rope and knew I'd reach the prize at the end of the adventure. It was all worth it.

5

THE COLD CALL AND
THE ART OF THE SCHMOOZE

———— • ————

Cold-calling, it sounds so harsh. It makes me think of trying to wake someone from a dead sleep, nudging them—"Hello, I'm here, you don't know me, but let me introduce myself and help your business." You are presenting yourself to someone and engaging in a conversation with an agenda—schmoozing to obtain more information about them. I'm a social person, so I like talking with strangers and figuring them out. But learning how to do it well can be a challenge.

I didn't realize the word schmooze is derived from Yiddish for *schmues*, or to talk. Schmooze is defined as chatting or conversing informally. But to me, it isn't just idle chatter. What the prospect thinks of as a casual exchange, I see as a prime way to gather information, all without seeming like you're trying to make a sale. The goal is to connect in a non-threatening way.

I discovered I had a knack for using the schmooze technique when I started cold-calling in my Washington, DC, sales job. I was at first overwhelmed when my manager handed me a colorful but complicated subway map and a list of businesses. Since I was new to the city, I had no contacts to start with, just a quadrant of the district on the map as my territory to conquer.

I started from scratch and built my client base by cold-calling every building I could get into—knocking on doors, leaving information, and schmoozing the receptionist for follow-up contacts. I walked and rode the metro everywhere and put a lot of mileage on my body. In the summer, the soles of my shoes melted from the one-hundred-degree sidewalks and streets between trips underground on the busy subway lines.

COLD-CALLING RULE #1

Know when to ignore the *No Soliciting* sign, and how to get past it.

The whoosh of the door when I entered office buildings always made me feel bold and powerful. Then, inevitably, I'd hear, "Whoa. Hold it, lady." And I would have to navigate the first gatekeepers.

Some lobbies had burly security guards, so unless you had an appointment, you couldn't get past them. I never fooled with those guys. They usually wore a badge and would probably post a photo of my face on the wall if I became one of "those" aggressive salespeople. I retreated in search of the many other buildings open to explore.

Signs on the business doors that said *No Soliciting* sometimes replaced security guards. Still, if I wanted to make a sale, I had to find ways to get around them.

Entering an office can take guts, especially under a sign that includes the word *no* on it. I would open the door, take a deep breath, smile, and prepare to engage the receptionist. On occasion,

I was told to leave the lobby area by those gatekeepers who had orders to be the meanest person on the planet to anyone walking in without an appointment, i.e., salespeople.

I heard phrases like, "Get out of here *now*, can't you read?" This was usually an indication that the *No Soliciting* sign really meant, "Entry into our little kingdom is closed and we have dragons ready to slay any intruders." The dragons were sometimes tamed by politely introducing myself: "I am providing information about a service, not soliciting." I would leave my card and ask who I could contact for an appointment (so I could be welcomed back in a more civilized way).

That schmooze tactic usually worked, and I rarely took it personally if I was told to leave immediately after handing over my card. At times, a very bored receptionist who complimented my outfit or felt sorry for me because I was having a bad hair day from walking in the steamy summer heat would strike up a conversation. These were the ice-breaker moments that created friendly conversation. I was schmoozing my way in. Before I knew it, I had an appointment, or the decision-maker's name for a follow-up call. You bet the receptionist will remember me with pleasure when I call back.

COLD-CALLING RULE #2

Know when to get out of the building.

Some offices were easier to enter than others. If there wasn't a receptionist sentry, sometimes I'd go knocking at the company doors throughout the building. But you have to know when to cut your losses if you can't get in because doors are locked, or you end up somewhere you're definitely not welcome.

My most memorable cold-call attempt was in a nondescript rambling building in Washington, DC. There are small embassies scattered in different areas around the city, and some have offices in mainstream buildings. This particular complex had some tiny country's embassy office on one floor in addition to several private businesses.

I remember walking down the dark hallway and trying locked doors. Suddenly I heard on a loudspeaker, hidden somewhere no doubt with a roving camera, "I see her. She's wearing a brown leather coat walking past the elevator." Knowing at that point that the embassy security was watching my every move, I decided the best thing to do was either put my hands up and face the rent-a-cops or leave quickly and calmly before I saw *Surrender Dorothy* in spray paint on the wall. There are ten thousand spies in the city, and I didn't want to be misidentified and unknowingly cause an international incident.

COLD-CALLING RULE #3

Always be prepared to make a full pitch, with blank agreements in your briefcase to seal the deal in the rare occasion a manager is available to meet with you.

Timing is everything. When I least expected it, I could walk out of a cold call with an appointment. Getting an on-the-spot introduction and meeting with a decision-maker was my top goal.

Being in the right place at the right time could be as easy as meeting a manager who happened to be talking with the receptionist when I walked in. Even better is entering an empty reception area and hearing voices from interior offices, enticing me to start wandering back there. My "Hello!" would perk up the unknowing victim with their door open, working at their desk. "There was no one out front and I wanted to introduce myself." I was entering the inner sanctum, which allowed me to be passed around to meet the manager.

Inevitably, if I was polite, the insider I met first was helpful. "Oh, I'm not the person you should talk to. Let me get Betty; she's the personnel manager who makes those decisions." Bingo, I'm in. I'm going to meet Betty, the decision-maker. Their gatekeeper was out to lunch, or quit, or worse, so now I'm getting to the manager I've been trying to reach on the phone for days.

"Betty," I said, "It looks like you need a receptionist. Let me help you with that." Betty says, "That agency we use sent me a dud—she didn't return after lunch, so I'm glad you came in because I'll never use that company again." I'd then return to my office with the receptionist order or have a follow-up meeting set to prevent this problem in the future. I couldn't help but feel my heart start to race while I envisioned those dancing commission dollar signs as the conversation would lead to a signed agreement.

COLD-CALLING RULE #4

Revive an unresponsive client with a schmoozy cold call.

Waking the dead—it's what one of my sales managers referred to as reviving an unresponsive client. Fast-forward a few years to a TV station I worked for as a new account rep. I was tasked with asking a former client to advertise again. It was an auto dealership and getting those accounts was like winning the lottery.

My sales manager said no other rep had been successful in getting the business back. The dealership general manager was a tough personality, unfriendly and cynical, a tough nut to crack. He would order a rep to leave because he didn't like his tie or something ridiculous like that. He was a legend.

Time for a new approach—I was going to kill him with kindness. Walking in without an appointment, like a cold call, caught the dreaded manager off guard. With a little schmoozing and saying with a smile I had a special offer that would help increase sales, he led me right back to his office.

He was a little gruff at first but after some discussion and negotiation, he signed the contract. He wanted to give the TV station a try again. I'd come just at the right time. As the process was unfolding, I kept thinking, *This can't be happening.* I was a nervous wreck on the inside and hoped he couldn't tell my face was flushing and my hands were shaking while I closed the deal. Suffice it to say, I was the hero of the day when I returned to the office waving the agreement. My surprise visit, friendly and cheerful, revived the dead account everyone else had given up on.

COLD-CALLING RULE #5

Don't bad-mouth the competition.

Let's face it, you know your product or service is the best, but always keep the competition out of it. It will never sweeten a sale and could sabotage your credibility.

When making cold calls by phone or visiting in person for the personnel agency, I would get the usual pushback: "We use ABC agency and are very happy with them." I would disarm them by saying, "They are a good company with a fine reputation. However, I know you would be pleased with the quality of our people. I'll be in your building on Tuesday; would you have a few minutes for me to stop by at ten o'clock to tell you how we can help when they can't?"

Affirming there is competition out there and then asking for the appointment can open the door to a nonthreatening new relationship. Bad-mouthing a competitor is bad business no matter whether you're cold-calling or talking with someone at a business card exchange.

COLD-CALLING RULE #6

Treat networking like a cold-call.

Those business card exchanges at local chambers of commerce are full of people eager to do business with you. Many people dread them, but I learned that good networking is just a cold-call schmoozing opportunity with an added bonus—a shared agenda to connect.

The successful salesperson knows the basics of Networking 101 and follows them:

Don't be late to the party. Arriving on time or early to a networking event allows you to meet people before they start forming groups or cliques that you can't break into.

Wear your name badge correctly. Don't make the prospect feel awkward (especially if you are a woman) by forcing them to look all over your chest for your name. Badge placement on the right side provides a direct line of sight to the person you are shaking hands with so they can remember your name.

Be prepared with a fifteen-second elevator speech. Tell people how you can help them solve their problems and hand them your business card.

Exchange business cards in a meaningful way. Leave the event with one to five quality leads and confirm a date and time and with whom you will be following up.

Follow-up the day after the event. They already told you to call, or you have asked permission to call. Now you have a mutual agreement to reconnect.

Schmooze with confidence. Attending these events is a lot like cold-calling—you meet someone, do a little schmoozing, and start developing a relationship. There are people in this world who excel at the art of schmoozing. At one of these events, a sales peer may say, "Oh, she's over there schmoozing," or "She's really good at schmoozing people." What is really being said is she is "laying on the charm" or getting someone into a comfortable conversation. Just make sure you show sincere interest. The conversation should lead to clues that are then acted upon for a follow-up meeting.

A good schmoozer should also be a great listener. "We were just awarded a huge grant for marketing," says the person you just met who can lead you to the decision-maker and some or all of those marketing dollars. This person is worth a follow-up. Pay attention, learn more, and be enthusiastic.

The interaction isn't all about you; it's about making connections with new people who may have value to you. The last thing someone wants to hear is detail about how you do your job and boring personal stories. Listening carefully for clues about what they care about can provide information that may reveal an opportunity.

And networking cold-call opportunities don't only happen at the chamber of commerce. When I sold advertising for a local magazine, I was once in a casual conversation with a friend at her retirement luncheon. Her friend's husband, who worked for a well-respected car dealership, was also there. After we were introduced and talking, he mentioned they would soon be celebrating one-hundred years in business. I made a mental note and followed up with him the next day. My eventual reconnection with him resulted in a large advertising commitment promoting their anniversary in the magazine.

It doesn't matter where you are, a business or personal event, there is always an opportunity for schmoozing and potential prospects from people you are with, people who may join your client list.

Schmooze to attract attention. I never felt more powerful than when I was at our chamber of commerce business mixers. At every turn, I knew someone or wanted to know someone. I would start talking, or should I say schmoozing, with someone I knew, and then another person I didn't know would join in. Then a small group would form, and introductions would start among those gathered and the circle would grow larger—everyone would start sharing information. It's the schmooze effect—growing your circle by being with people who want to be actively engaged.

Don't be afraid to open a circle of colleagues and potential clients. Effective schmoozing creates openers for business relationships. Be curious and friendly, and it will eventually attract the people you need to meet.

Schmooze with integrity—they want to know the expert. I love watching a pro schmoozer in action. For example, Dave is a respected landscaper in town. How do I know that? He shows up to every event in his own company's professional uniform. He knows how to schmooze and engage in casual conversations. People will ask him questions about his business, and he will tell them how he can help. He has become the expert and the go-to person for landscaping.

Be the face of your business and other experts will introduce you as "someone you need to know." When people get to know what you do and your look reflects your profession, soon you'll be known as the trusted expert in your field. You will be sought after. And you can connect an expert to another person you meet and become their hero by introducing them as someone who could solve their problem, thus strengthening your relationship and making future connections even stronger.

When I moved on from my sales job at the chamber of commerce, some members couldn't believe I was leaving. They all said something like: "But you *are* the chamber; do they realize what they're losing?" That was very humbling, and it made me feel valued. They knew I was the expert they could count on. I turned those members who appreciated me into supporters for my next sales job, and they continued to help connect me to customers, with a few becoming loyal clients as well for my new employer.

Schmoozing follow-up—keep up with your new contacts. You just schmoozed a bridge—use it, don't lose it! You put a lot of effort into schmoozing and developing relationships. Even if you don't currently do business with a colleague, they will bring business to you in the future. I had some business acquaintances who could not use the product I was currently selling but liked what I had to offer when I moved on to a new job, or when they changed jobs.

While working for a magazine, some of my clients wanted more than print advertising—perhaps digital or video. When I worked for television, video was the attraction for those magazine clients who wanted to diversify their ad campaigns. They liked working with me before and wanted to continue that relationship in my new job because I offered them something they needed, and they trusted me to listen and make sure they were satisfied.

People do business with someone they know and trust. Your value grows the more others get to know you. That first conversation can open the door to a follow-up meeting, with social and professional relationships developing as you continue to connect.

Be confident and own the schmooze. Everyone starts out as a stranger whether they're cold-calling or new to a networking group. Be the person who is actively engaged and gets leads while making friends. You'll then be remembered and looked upon as their trusted advisor and expert in your field.

6

GETTING TO YES: WHY PEOPLE LIE IN A SALES NEGOTIATION

When I was growing up, my mother used a pressure cooker to prepare food. It was the heaviest metal pot in our kitchen, with an equally heavy lid and a valve on top. She would add the food and water to the pot, cover it, and wait for the sound of steam to whistle out of the narrow valve. A heavy metal cap was placed on the valve, stopping the pressure buildup. When the pressure leveled off, the food was cooked, and then the lid was removed revealing a perfect meal. It was amazing how that pot worked. If the steps weren't followed to stop the pressure, mom said the pot would explode. No wonder she never let us touch it.

Many years later, I found that a pressure cooker and the sales process are in fact related. There's a process to winning and if all the ingredients are there it's quite a complicated buildup getting to *yes*. The ingredients are added to the pot—the relationship, presentation, and potential deal. The lid closes, and the pressure starts rising. There's whistling and steam while the prospect considers the offer. The anticipation of securing the deal is relieved when the lid is removed, revealing a perfectly cooked win.

The first step in the win process is presenting the product—a membership to the chamber of commerce, an office, a temporary employee, a magazine ad, or a commercial on TV. Whatever I was presenting had to satisfy a need for the prospect—using a kitchen tool for family meals, having an office to run a business, bringing in more customers with advertising—all providing a solution to a problem.

How I present a solution to solve their problem is the heart of a presentation. I've found that no matter what you're selling, the same sales techniques can be used in most presentations and for closing the deal.

Before the presentation, always check the company website revealing what they do, produce, or sell—a.k.a. the "widget." Know who you're talking to and review their profile on LinkedIn. Make sure you understand their "pain" level or why they asked for your help so you can provide a solution. Then follow these steps.

SELLING TO WIN TECHNIQUE #1

Assess and tailor the presentation to the need.

What does the client need? Is it more customers? To make a certain number of sales per year? To hire more employees? To present the right product, ask the right questions. Some examples include: How many widgets do you need to sell to make a profit in one month? How many employees do you need to hire to make monthly quotas? Who is your ideal customer?

Using a client needs analysis (CNA) template, asking specific questions will address the problems they're having, which makes the presentation more effective. Ideally, the questions should be discussed in advance so that solutions can be provided during the meeting. When the needs analysis can't be done in advance, ask the questions at the meeting—preferably as close to the beginning as possible; you don't want to run out of time.

Watch out for a prospect that's trying to hijack your question session. When I was selling office space, I met with some small-business owners who had huge egos. They couldn't stop talking about themselves and how they built their little empires. Their stories were interesting, but details that weren't pertinent to our meeting just took up time. Keep the conversation on track by agreeing to the time limit of the meeting, and gently leading the prospect through the sales process.

I found that some people have no intention of buying in the first place and just want to hear themselves talk. That's when having the needs analysis done in advance is helpful to control the conversation and the sales process—be ready to present the solution to the need without wasting time with small talk opening the door to their distractions. Of course there's always schmoozing, but you need to honor the prearranged purpose of the sales meeting and your mutual professional time commitment.

SELLING TO WIN TECHNIQUE #2

Make the prospect feel the love.

The best way to show your love of their business is to be a customer yourself. That means you already have a relationship with their company, as a consumer. It makes you more authentic and valuable as a salesperson in their eyes.

For example, I enjoyed eating at a particular restaurant, and went there often. After dining, I asked to see the manager or owner so I could rave about the awesome burger and the great customer service I just had. Then I requested a meeting to talk about advertising. Adding a little extra emotion and gushing to them about my experience as a customer showed I was passionate about their food and their business.

After meeting and presenting the campaign for their magazine advertising, they knew my enthusiasm for their business would translate into great service, which I provided to them as my new client.

Some of my best restaurant accounts for magazine advertising started with me as their raving fan. Two restaurants landed on the magazine's covers. One was so happy that they framed and displayed it in their dining room and told me how much they loved *me*. They became my best customers and it all started with showing my appreciation for their food that I loved so much.

SELLING TO WIN TECHNIQUE #3

Like what you sell.

Every product has strengths and flaws. Knowing your product and selling its strengths helps the client buy what works for them.

While selling office space, my presentation was a company-generated slick video that painted a very rosy picture of the offices and services we provided. But at what cost? You could rent an office with a desk and two chairs at a great price—but there were no windows. Want windows? Pay more. Want a phone? Pay more. Want someone to answer your phone? Pay more.

There were extra charges for everything, and some prospects would question them. I knew most of the charges were worth the cost, if it gave the customer what they needed. But I grew to dislike having to defend what I call "nickel-and-diming" schedules. I found myself thinking about how much I agreed with their objections. What I really wanted to say was that the pricing was a little high, but we could probably find a solution they could afford without buying all the extras. Of course, that's not what the company hoped for. I knew about the add-ons, but if they couldn't afford them, I could sell them the office space without those. Just to keep them engaged and trusting so I wouldn't lose the sale, I learned to refocus on the charges. I was able to convince them they would still be happy with what they could afford, saying, "You have a cell phone, so you don't need one on your desk. You just saved fifty dollars a month."

SELLING TO WIN TECHNIQUE #4

Don't get hijacked by your own manager.

Sometimes managers want to be included in the process of presenting and closing. I preferred to close on my own because it kept me in charge of the relationship I had created with the prospect. Adding new personalities at the end can throw off the vibe and momentum.

One of my bosses reworked an entire final presentation the way he thought I should pitch it, essentially telling the prospect how to run his business. The prospect didn't like that. He abruptly walked out of the room while my manager was presenting graphs, pie charts, cost-benefit ratios, and other compelling evidence *he* thought was important. It was obvious the prospect was agitated and when he came back to the room, he looked at us and said, "Okay, I know you think we're doing everything wrong, you've made your case. But why are you suddenly bringing all this up?"

We didn't get the deal because my manager didn't understand what the prospect wanted. He hijacked my presentation. He said he wanted to help me learn how to be better at sales, and change me by applying his techniques that work for him. What he didn't do was ask what my strategies were and how I wanted to apply them to the presentation. He didn't consider my understanding of the prospect's needs.

The momentum I had created was ruined and I had to start all over again. I eventually won the business back, but after months of persistent calls and meetings. In the end, my initial prospect left the company and I had to wait for the sale when a new decision-maker was hired. I redeveloped a relationship, presented a solution to their problem, and gained them as a new client.

SELLING TO WIN TECHNIQUE #5

Close like you expect it.

The presentation should lead directly to the close. Visualize the prospect saying *yes*, and you'll be more confident. So will they.

I tend to nod my head when asking, "Are we ready to move forward today?" Or I ask, "What other questions do you have before we get started with the agreement?" Or, "Is next Monday a good starting date for you?"

Conversely, when the expectation for a *yes* turns out to be a *no*, know that something's up. Ask, what's causing this response? Is it an unanswered question that needs clarification? Have they been lying to me all along about their interest in my product? Being sure you've covered all the bases so there's no uncertainty is very important.

The challenge in the sales process is when you *assume* you've sold them because they say to you, "Oh, yes, I'm definitely interested." Behind that interest are often hidden hesitations and intentions. Is their true intention to buy or are they lying, politely leading you on for their own reasons? Whether they intentionally lie or just can't give a straight answer, it can be frustrating.

Be aware of the lying techniques the buyer will use. For example, some promise to buy next year or ask for a follow-up that will make no real difference in their decision. ("Call me in a week.") Of course, you can never reach them again. It's a familiar complaint we would share among our sales teams—we just wanted a yes-or-no answer so we can all move on.

After all the effort I put into this process, don't string me along if you really don't want to buy my product. Saying, "This may not be a good fit for either of us," could lead to a deeper discussion of what the problem is, or a friendly agreement that the deal really may not be a good fit. Both the salesperson and the prospect will feel better about the conversation, and that opens up the potential for an ongoing relationship. That's when you ask for a referral. Who do they know would benefit from the services you're selling?

LYING TROUBLESHOOTING TECHNIQUE #1

Decision-Maker Dilemma.

I call this strategy the "I have to talk it over with my wife or husband first" put off.

Of course, this could be a true excuse, because the spouse knows making their own decision could result in divorce. Buying decisions vary greatly between family-owned and corporate businesses. The family-owned decision is usually a joint one.

But sometimes, it's a lie that hides a reason they're hesitating. Do they still have questions or are all buying decisions actually mutually agreed to? In these cases, in my experience, it seems some men won't make the decision on their own. "She makes all the decisions" was a common response and an indicator of who wore the pants in the imaginary family the prospect is creating to distract you from the real problem.

Always treat their statement as the truth, though, and move forward to explore possible solutions. If they have questions that remain unanswered, or if there are issues you don't know about, find out in a friendly way, and clarify things as you go. In the event the prospect truly needs input from their spouse or partner, then ask, "What questions do you think they may have before moving forward? I can address those now so you will be prepared to answer them."

If they don't know their partner well enough to tell you, then it's probably a stall tactic. In any case, when someone uses this excuse, it's best to set up another appointment with both decision-makers present.

LYING TROUBLESHOOTING TECHNIQUE #2

"I have to think about it."

This stall tactic happens in every sales situation, almost verbatim: "Yes, I'm interested but have to think about it."

You've done everything you can to get to *yes*—answered any objections, worked with them on price, etc., and now must set up a follow-up call. You mutually agree to the date before the meeting ends—you now have their permission to contact them for an answer.

Making that call can be stressful—you feel confident it will be a *yes*, but you must be prepared for a *no*. I ask, "So, are we ready to move forward?" Waiting those few seconds for an answer can seem like an eternity. And then you'll often get a flat-out *no*. It's a real blow when you've been through the whole process, think they are ready to sign or buy and can't believe they may have lied to you about their interest in buying. They could be unsure or still have unanswered questions, but to you it feels like a lie because you thought they wanted your product.

Maybe it wasn't a good fit today, but it may be in the future. I've turned this kind of delayed *no* around by checking back in a few months and being pleasantly surprised that my first contact left the company or someone else is handling those decisions. That's a great opportunity to start a new relationship with someone who may now say *yes*.

The psychological truth is that most people just feel bad about saying *no*. They may have had no intention of buying in the first place; they just wanted to shop around for a future decision. Or they may fear getting buyer's remorse—feeling guilty for spending the money after the sale.

As a former sales manager of mine would say, telling the prospect before the presentation that *no* is an okay answer lifts some of the pressure if they feel bad they can't get to *yes*. In general, setting clear expectations before the presentation about this and other steps forward with the prospect will put them more at ease. Chances are when they say *yes*, they'll feel better about it, and they'll stick with you and your company.

LYING TROUBLESHOOTING TECHNIQUE #3

"It's too expensive."

When I was working for a TV station, many prospects not familiar with television advertising costs would often say they can't buy because TV is just too expensive. When I asked what they *thought* it would cost, their guess was so unrealistically high I knew they had been influenced by some competitor or had bad information.

My response to a concern about being too expensive is often, "What is expensive to you?" Alternatively, I link discussions about cost to the value of the package. I ask: "What do you think is reasonable for all I am offering to you in this package?" At this point, the prospect is surprised you've asked questions and are interested in their thoughts. They were planning to just walk out the door with the "too expensive" excuse and be done with you. It's a tactic that has worked for them in the past. Some of them are probably bargain hunters with no intent to buy. But maybe they don't need all the bells and whistles right away and can sign a contract that gives them what they need for the price they can afford.

Educate them on the value of what they're buying and its benefits. Ask, "Can we negotiate on price and come to a mutual agreement?" This way the sale is not lost and there is still a deal being made. As the client works with you, if your customer service is strong, the benefits of a long-term commitment from this client are much greater than if there was no deal at all.

Learning some techniques to maintain your confidence as you overcome and face the onslaught of objections and uncertainty will help get you through some of the challenges of selling. Dealing with the pressure cooker of sales is not easy. But, if you know that these elements are what every salesperson must overcome, it may be a little more reassuring. You're not in the pressure cooker alone.

Follow the steps to avoid a possibly explosive situation, and keep that valve under control—anticipate objections, be ready to answer questions, and have confidence in your skills—because in the end you'll have a delectable deal to savor for yourself and the new client.

7

MYTHS, TRUTHS, AND LEGENDS: THE UNIQUE WORLD OF HOME-BASED BUSINESS SALES

———•———

One of the most educational sales jobs I ever had was my time as a Pampered Chef (PC) home-based, "part-time" kitchen consultant. I'll never forget some of the lessons I learned, and the conversations I had, as I navigated house parties and other domestic adventures.

I started my home-based products experiences as a customer. "My husband would divorce me if he knew how much I paid for this basket," one well-coiffed, earnest housewife once said at a house party where I was a guest. With no spouses in sight, this was a common lament repeated by women purchasing these unique baskets during a home show while sitting in the safety and comfort of their neighbor's living room. But the attraction of the basket was often as strong as the fear of a husband's anger. (According to my friend's husband who is an attorney, these specially made and individually signed baskets are so coveted and collected, they show up in prenuptial agreements.)

I must have hundreds of dollars worth of merchandise from companies whose products like these were displayed at house parties I attended over the years. Jewelry, fine crystal, toys, Tupperware, kitchen products, home decor items, baskets of every shape and size, and pottery are still in my home. Some are displayed but most are either boxed up or rarely used. Don't get me wrong—I am not against home parties or the products they spread throughout America. It's just that I've been on both sides, and I believe it's important to be aware of the truth behind the promises, myths, and legends.

I first attended these parties to support my friends, who, as consultants, believed the myth they could have it all by staying home with the kids and running a business to make extra money to supplement their family's income. But owning your own business can come with a heavy price. It's called *stress*.

Sure, there are regular customers hooked on the product line, who always had to have the newest release. Some, like me, just wanted to be supportive and bought something useful, like a sixty-five-dollar specialty berry basket for gathering fruit at a farm. We were told by the consultant that the berry-picking experience just wouldn't be the same if a tacky plastic grocery bag was used instead of a fashionable basket. Whether we had a farm or not, we wanted an authentic experience, or imagined we did, even though I bought fruit at the grocery store. I resisted the expensive basket, unlike the guilty woman I quoted above.

But I became one of those avid customers when I discovered PC products. It seemed the natural next step to start selling them. Desperately seeking adult contact away from home and looking to make extra money, I approached my friend about becoming a sales rep. Since I had left the workforce four years earlier to raise my children, I felt I still had an obligation to contribute to the household income.

My husband never pressured me to work, but he did appreciate whatever I could add to the pot since we were raising a family. PC also promised I could have a satisfying part-time job where I could continue to build my sales and public-speaking skills. Plus, I would have something to fill my résumé during my stay-at-home-mom years.

I did like to cook and would enjoy presenting kitchen tools that I already loved. I was ready to reach for that dangling PC super scraper and two-quart batter bowl—essentials for any kitchen— and step out of the audience into the sales spotlight. I felt I would be part of something big and fulfilling.

I plunked down my one-hundred dollars for the "starter kit." It had every kitchen "tool" (not *gadget,* that's a no-no term in the PC biz) necessary to start a business. We would demonstrate the products in a host home (on the kitchen or dining room table surrounded by chairs) filled with eager PC junkies who wanted to sample food I prepared with all those helpful tools you couldn't find anywhere else.

The "kit" was in a *heavy* wooden crate. Eventually, as we acquired more tools to demonstrate, we would carry the gear in large luggage-type bags, but they were still heavy. My husband usually had to carry and load the awkward crate or luggage into my minivan for the "shows" I would travel to. And, back in the '90s and early 2000s there was no GPS to help with directions to a home that was off the beaten path in the middle of the woods at the other end of the county.

Once I arrived, after not knowing how I got there, I could always tell if the husband or significant other at the host home was the greatest guy ever or just wanted to watch me struggle with all my stuff. Would he help me get the fifty-pound collection of heavy baking stones, frying pans, and glass bowls packed in a wooden crate out of my van? I was relieved when any able-bodied man, or woman, would help me haul the heavy items into the house. But I also learned to carry my own gear when help wasn't available. It was part of the job.

As a mother myself, I had young mother friends in a brand-new development so getting started in this type of business was a no-brainer. My friends were very supportive. And that's how running a business like PC had been successful for most women. I started with a small circle and branched out of the neighborhood rather quickly.

My husband's job was thirty miles from our home so at least two nights per week I would literally hand off my infant son to him and my toddler daughter just as he walked in the door. I was relieved I could get on the road and to my adoring PC fans on time.

I was still nursing, and I had to schedule my son's last feeding so his tummy would be full until I got home. I remember my husband being a wreck over worrying about that. I would always assure him that everything would be fine, and the kid would not starve before I returned (fuss and cry maybe, but not starve). What I had to worry about was covering up embarrassing milk leakage stains with a PC apron while beating eggs at warp speed with a wire whisk.

HOME-BASED BUSINESS MYTH #1

Home-based businesses let you "have it all" by becoming your own boss on your terms.

Don't believe everything you hear about all the benefits of a home-based business, especially during vulnerable times in your life, e.g., while starting a family or in a tough family transition.

Selling wares for a home-based business sounds so easy in the brochure, but you must consider what you're getting yourself into for the long term. The myths can be so distracting from the truth that home-based sales are rarely as part-time or as conveniently compartmentalized as you wish they were.

That is, the benefits of entrepreneurship for you will go beyond the satisfying performances of product demonstrations. You'll also have to plan for isolating yourself away from the family when you're doing paperwork, making phone calls, and scheduling parties— plus managing your time to go out and sell, and scheduling enough "kitchen shows" to meet your personal goals. If you don't want to do these regular business tasks, then you need to think twice about being your own boss. We as women often brag about multitasking, but not everyone can "have it all" and handle more responsibilities without adding more stress to our lives.

Finally, it must be said: your business will also be home-based (hint: a code word for *it's in your house*). That means it's with you 24/7, even when you close your office door (if you're lucky enough to have one).

If I were to write a how-to-be-a-Pampered Chef-consultant instruction book, I'd say there are real benefits to working from home and selling a product you value—but it takes a lot of work to find success. Success requires having an understanding husband or partner who is not demanding of your time and can take care of the kids while you're out selling for an entire evening. I was lucky. My husband was great in that way. That's just the reality of it; both parents are in this together.

HOME-BASED BUSINESS MYTH #2

The rewards will come automatically. Get out of the house a couple days a week, earn lots of extra money, and win incentive trips to Disney with your family!

Who doesn't want to be the hero to their kids, buy them great toys for the holidays, and win a vacation? Earning those bonuses sounded so perfect and so easy. Just sell some kitchen tools—but wait—a trip to Disney comes with requirements—selling thousands of dollars worth of products in a few months' time? And that was just a trip for two, let alone bringing my kids along.

I wanted to believe the myth. Who wouldn't want to believe the perks were just a sales pitch away? Have it all with a part-time job, raise my kids, make extra money, and see Mickey and Minnie for free (BTW airfare not included). It sounded like the best of all worlds and a great way to add to the home income.

I thought I could win that Disney vacation by selling the products I loved, until I did the math. To qualify, I would have to do ten shows per month multiplied by $1,000 in sales per show. That means selling five $250 cookware sets to five people, or selling ten pizza cutters, eight baking stones, twelve batter bowls, fifteen super scrapers, one cookware set, and ten cheese graters to twelve people to win the trip. Considering most shows averaged about $600, selling mega amounts of product to earn a trip for just *two* people was a lofty goal to reach.

I was confident that once I became a more experienced seller, I could win that trip another year so the kids could come. That is, if I could have it all by keeping up my sales pace, plus helping with homework, doing the laundry, shopping for groceries, cleaning the house, making dinner, and then finding time to actually *go* on a vacation. Ultimately, I never earned the Disney trip, but all my efforts were rewarded with a fun trip to Montreal with my family and a leadership trip to New Orleans. We enjoyed these wins, even though they required a lot of time and sales effort to meet the goals to qualify.

HOME-BASED BUSINESS MYTH #3

You can advance to director quickly by building your team, thus making passive income for you and your family.

That was the incentive carrot dangled by the consultant who invites prospective sales reps to join any multilevel marketing company. The not-so-secret goal of multilevel business structures is to recruit consultants to increase your downline and become a director.

I probably sold a literal ton of kitchen tools during my seven-year career with PC. (Yes, seven years—and I don't regret the commitment, even though I had to moderate my expectations of getting rich quickly.) My client base was exploding, and I added a few kitchen consultants to my downline so I could advance to director. But the new consultants were needy and some lacked the initiative to sell. I started to feel like a babysitter. I already had kids at home. Did I need more? The bottom line—if they didn't sell, I didn't make more money on their sales to add to my commission. I had to become their mentor—and that's not passive income.

Most PC product lovers wanted to become a consultant to get the starter kit for products at a reduced rate. To them, selling the products was secondary. In fact, many new consultants had no sales experience and were just looking to make some quick extra money without much effort and enjoy the products they had just bought. Trying to recruit the right people turned out to be a challenge. Some would sign up and quit—leaving with about $250 worth of kitchen products for a $100 investment. Others would just linger in my downline, justifying my "director" title but nothing more.

I'll admit it. I didn't like recruiting. Selling was much more rewarding to me. I envied one of my consultant peers who had perfected her recruitment strategy. She would share her emotional story about almost losing their family farm if it were not for the money she earned as a kitchen consultant. She seemed so heroic. Who wouldn't want to join her team? Other consultants told stories about being a lonely mom at home who never thought they had any value after putting their careers on hold, saying how their lives improved dramatically as kitchen consultants. Whether these stories were true or not, as expected, the audience would be teary-eyed, and noticeably emotionally involved in their stories. A few signed up because they felt just like those consultants—hungry for value or called to help their families out of financial problems.

But my story wasn't that compelling. And I needed sellers not emotional wrecks. I couldn't tell those guaranteed-recruitment stories because they weren't mine. I thought about making some up like that, but I didn't feel like that would be genuine, and being authentic always worked better for me in sales. I believe people eventually see through manipulations and exaggerations.

One thing I did learn was to be a successful director, you need to build a strong team with people who have their hearts in it and want to sell. So, over time I zeroed in on women who were passionate about the products. Those who were oohing and aahing, kissing and caressing that pizza stone. They didn't realize that their enthusiasm was already selling the products they loved to their friends sitting right next to them. They could be very successful with little training.

So, these sounded like perfect recruits, right? "You would be a great consultant," I'd say. But then I'd get responses like, "I'm not a salesperson" or "I could never do what you do." Was I looking too professional and not acting like an average person? I did feel confident and pretty successful at this point. Maybe they perceived me as highly trained or something. Maybe they never sold Girl Scout Cookies or felt like they were "Thumbody" and won a prize. Whatever their reluctance, they thought they couldn't do what I did. I thought I must have given them the wrong message. Or maybe, like so many women, they just needed some confidence like I had to do this.

My pushy upline director kept encouraging me to build my team. I was happy enough to sell these quality products and make money from the tremendous book of business I had created over the years. Yes, I was successful, but I'd designed my PC success by building on my personal and professional goals.

She held a new carrot out: if I pushed myself further, I could be invited to the national conference, and stand on the stage with her, as she celebrated our teamwork and got her executive director award. I pushed until I had recruited five consultants and needed only one more to sign up to qualify as a director. My last recruit needed to submit her paperwork before a deadline that was only days away. She didn't seem as excited as I was about making her decision to join up so quickly. Enthusiastic, and even though I knew she would probably never step up and sell products, I got her to send in her application just in time to attend the big annual conference in Chicago.

It was only when I watched my upline director get a huge ovation for her promotion that I realized that all she wanted was to move up to the next level and had used the same pushy tactics with all her downline directors. She said she was doing this for my benefit so I could be recognized at the conference, but in the fading afterglow of the group-presentation applause for my achievement, I had an epiphany.

I realized her big moment was only because of my forcing someone to sign up as a consultant who really didn't want to, and who wouldn't add to my team. It wasn't all about me; it was all about *her* getting the big promotion. She had acted without *my* business at heart. I realized I had acted the same way with my new consultant who signed and sent the agreement in time for *me* to get the status I thought I wanted. I was turning into my overly aggressive used-car-salesman inauthentic nemesis. I had been caught up in the hype.

No big surprise: when I returned home, the new consultant quit. She had felt forced into joining and didn't want to sell. All that recruiting work for nothing. I found another person to add to my team, but after a few months she decided the physical demands of hauling around heavy stoneware and kitchen tools were too much for her. I was sad for her because I knew she loved the products. She quit and sold Avon and became quite successful at it. Those products seemed light as a feather in comparison.

LEGENDARY DIRECTOR MYTH

Anyone can become a high-level executive director and have their picture and story in the company catalog.

As kitchen consultants, most of us longed to have our names and photos appear in the company's catalog as high achievers. Who doesn't want to be famous? They all had the best life stories and successes to tell. We had hopes and dreams of being those legendary consultants one day.

The top-tier achievers seemed to be a fortunate few who were willing to go above and beyond to be successful. They represented a small percentage of the hundreds of consultants who worked for the company. If being a high achiever was our goal, we soon found that a part-time effort wouldn't get us close to that level of fame.

I kept to my strengths, selling products I valued, bringing in money for my family, and gaining enjoyable experiences. As the years went by, I felt comfortable with my success. I didn't need to be one of those spotlighted people. I was content with reaching my personal sales goals, based on balancing my family time and my business.

To this day, I still meet people who can't place me or where we've met. I usually say, "Was I in your kitchen demonstrating kitchen tools to your friends?" That's when the light bulb goes off and we nod in agreement. They would tell me that they enjoyed having me as their consultant and how much they loved getting free products for hosting a show. That brought me a lot of satisfaction.

Building trust is a big part of selling and if you can gain the customers' trust and show passion for the products, your clients will remember you as the expert that brought value and quality. I realized being a company superstar or legend was not that important to me. I could become my own legend as a contributor to the family household income and as a respected "kitchen consultant" who commandeered a stranger's kitchen to sell products people loved. I never made a fortune as a kitchen consultant/director but the experience helped keep my sales skills sharp so I could be better prepared to reenter the workforce with more confidence.

HOME-BASED BUSINESS TRUTH #1

The company's yearly conferences and sales training classes will help you succeed.

Even though the award thrill at the convention was eventually kind of a disappointment for me, I was able to take a lot of quality training sessions the company provided for consultants with little sales experience or who needed more help to build their businesses.

In these trainings, new products were presented to the oohs and aahs of kitchen consultants in the audience—the enhanced ice cream scooper with the magical antifreeze fluid inside and the hard-anodized aluminum nonstick skillet with a lifetime guarantee. They were the newest, best, and truly innovative. We knew our customers would love them. Not to mention, who wouldn't want that dream Disney vacation if you could sell hundreds of those scoopers and skillets plus some mixing bowls?

I did learn some great selling techniques while attending training workshops at the conferences. To this day, I found that techniques used to sell my vast array of kitchen products—upselling, using affirmative phrases, addressing objections, using urgency to close—have all helped in other selling situations.

Of course, each of these workshops also aimed at getting me to believe the myths that would make me work harder, earning and distributing more products. When I was able to let go of those myths, I had more success in sales. Ultimately, I took what worked for me and kept growing my client list my own way. I learned that the key to my success was maximizing my own gifts and goals. It wasn't taking on the company's identity, except for maintaining friendly and professional expertise in the product.

HOME-BASED BUSINESS TRUTH #2

When choosing to be a home-based business consultant, sign up with a reputable company with quality products that people love.

I chose Pampered Chef because I knew they carried quality products that were obviously valuable to the home cook and well-made.

There were a lot of adoring PC fans who would rush me at the door of the home show asking what the newest and best "kitchen tools" were. When a product is high quality, and you just help enhance it with your personality and honesty, you can do very well in a business like this. It also helped that cooks like moms and dads needed these products so they could prepare meals and be heroes to their families. It was a little bit like selling those cookies; they know the brand and they have a need to satisfy with a proven product. And with PC, the products were demonstrated right before their eyes. That was fun.

I did a cute routine with the pizza cutter at my shows. The cutter was so big that you could see your face reflected in the mirror-like metal wheel. I would say, "When you're preparing dinner and the UPS guy shows up at the door, take a quick face scan on the pizza cutter to check your lipstick or makeup." A corny joke like this appealed to the moms who were starved for adult contact after being home with the kids all day. And why not add another practical use for buying that pizza cutter?

The job of selling tangible items was something new for me. Except for Girl Scout Cookies, I had only sold services before that you couldn't touch and feel. I'd return home at night in my minivan with the wooden crate filled with used kitchen tools, reeking of garlic and Parmesan cheese, which were frequent ingredients in the recipes I demonstrated. Not to mention scraping baked-on crescent roll dough off baking stones, because we used those rolls as a base for almost every recipe we would make. You could cut and chop any ingredient—fruits, vegetables, meats—and arrange it on a buttery bed of crescent roll dough, bake it, and serve it as an appetizer, entrée, or dessert. I should have bought stock in that dough company.

My day was not done until I finished washing the tools, stoneware, and bowls as the clock struck midnight. Usually everyone was tucked into their beds by then. I was still energized because I may have had a super successful $1,000 show or a $600 show and booked four more from the group that night. I did well, helped pay the mortgage, and enjoyed my job.

Who would have thought learning the techniques to sell measuring cups and spatulas would sharpen my sales skills for the future? I did—that's why I joined in the first place. I also made money that I needed and felt good about my contribution to the household finances. I became the Pampered Chef expert to my customers and a confident salesperson.

8

GREAT JOB!
NOW SELL MORE!

I n sales, it's always *never enough*. Just when you think you've reached your goal and had a great month, the tables turn, and the game starts over. Management always has bigger ideas about their sales team's performance.

I was so excited when I started bringing in business at my first job. I told my boss about my success, and he said, without fanfare, "That's what I hired you to do."

I'll admit I was surprised I wasn't recognized and awarded another "I'm Thumbody!" mug, or better yet, a bonus. I quickly realized I wasn't eleven and selling cookies anymore. Over the years, I learned to be careful what I wished for, because once you're recognized as a top performer, you're almost always awarded with more work.

What my boss at the personnel agency did expect was that I would serve the company where he saw fit. He wanted bigger things from me. After my first year, I proved I was able to consistently bring in new clients and was asked to open and manage a second office. It meant leaving the clients I had cultivated and loved. I had been rewarded with a bigger challenge. In some ways, that was good for me. In others, it led me dangerously close to burnout.

There I was, starting all over with conquering a new territory, and seeking out new business, all while maintaining an office staff. This was my "reward" for doing my job well. Little did I know I would be "rewarded" again in a similar way at future jobs. I rolled up my sleeves and got to work, looking for adventure.

Years later, when I worked at the chamber of commerce, the sales team was tasked with increasing the number of business memberships for the big one-hundred-year anniversary celebration. Leading up to that goal, the sales reps went above and beyond signing on new members to make that happen and the one-thousand-membership goal was exceeded. Telling the new members we wanted them to be part of our big year was a great selling point. We were so excited to be recognized for our stellar achievement at the big anniversary party.

The gala event arrived, and most of the members were in attendance plus local dignitaries to witness the anticipated congratulatory remarks. The CEO made his announcements and acknowledged that the one-thousand-member goal had not only been reached but exceeded. Then he said, "Now the sales team needs to go out and get even more members this year."

He didn't recognize us individually with anything, let alone a corny mug for our efforts. But the sales team knew how much work we put into reaching our goal, and we high-fived ourselves, celebrating our achievement. I figured if management didn't see the true value of my work, then my next employer will. It was another success story I added to my résumé.

After the big event, we all felt our sales success at the chamber was untouchable, and we prepared to match or exceed it using the strategies that had worked before. Then the VP announced, "We want to make you Superhuman Sellers." It may not have been those exact words, but that's how I felt when he said we were getting more training.

And he'd found a sales expert to teach us everything we needed to know to become superhuman. Before long, we were immersed in an intensive sales training course. After we slogged through the "sell this way" mind meld, which changed everything we've ever learned with new techniques, we went out on the streets and the entire team's sales tanked.

The new techniques just broke our concentration and momentum. We'd had success selling our own way. I had already developed my confidence in selling the service and schmoozing my networks. The old adage "If it ain't broke, don't fix it" proved true once more.

Further along in my career when I was selling office space, I had another success. I'd booked 93 percent of the offices within eighteen months at my location. I'd even managed "the big flood," which threatened to undo all my hard work bringing in tenants.

I left my office on a Friday after a "plumber" (and I use that term loosely) fixed a water pipe under the counter in the kitchen. What I didn't know was that he was an apprentice who had no business fixing anything by himself. Overnight, water leaked from the pipe connection into our offices and through the floor to the restaurant below.

I learned quickly how to handle those restoration companies who want to gouge you for tearing out walls to mitigate water and mold damage. Fortunately, I had a savvy building manager who helped me make the right decisions. We didn't have to tear out any walls, but we did have a lot of water damage.

The challenge for me was finding ways to gently step around dehumidifier fans while showing otherwise beautiful offices to prospects, simultaneously explaining that this type of disaster didn't usually happen. I found that every location this company ran had its own facility and maintenance issues to deal with. Spending more time fixing things cut into my sales work, but I kept focused.

Soon I was sitting on top of my little empire with happy clients and then I got the pat-on-the-back phone call from my executive director. She was so impressed with my achievements, she told me I would be transferred to manage the new office down the road in the next county.

Some pat on the back. I knew that office location was not performing, and the current sales manager was failing. I was so happy where I was that I asked if this was voluntary. Why would I want to travel an hour away and start all over again? She said, "Let's see how things go for six months."

She made this move sound like I was taking a car for a long test-drive. I could bring it back to the garage if I didn't want it. So, I agreed to it, thinking it would be temporary and if I didn't like it, I could return to my beloved office where I had been excelling. I understood that I had no choice but to go there or maybe lose my job.

I also knew I should feel flattered because I was asked to bring my expertise to the new location where they had just fired the manager. He evidently couldn't handle the pressure to bring in new clients. But I really was thinking, "Great, drop me into the cauldron of chaos so I can stir the pot and make everything better."

My manager made the task even more impossible, from the beginning. Not only was I assigned one fledgling office property to manage but a second one eleven miles away was scheduled to open soon. Red flags with the word *stress* in giant letters were popping up right in front of me and I ignored them. I looked at it as a new challenge I was going to conquer and confidently put on an "I'll show them what I can do" attitude.

To top it off, all the area sales managers were called back to our monthly meetings in the windowless basement classroom in a concrete parking garage that we called "the war room." There, we had meetings, sales training, and mediocre coffee in an effort to motivate us to sell more. Management would generally start meetings by reminding us we were never quite as good as we thought. Our artillery was in the form of laptops carried under our arms in protective bags. While we didn't wear military uniforms, the dress code was business suits and black was preferred. We looked more like Secret Service agents reporting for duty to an undisclosed location.

Maybe the term "sales jail" would better describe the experience akin to being sentenced to a room of solitary confinement with food and water handed to us through a small opening in the door. To earn the "Get Out Of Jail Free" card, we had to make dozens of calls, set appointments, and close any open deals. Maybe we should have been wearing orange inmate uniforms instead of the black suits.

And don't forget role playing—taking turns selling to the prospect in front of the entire group. This activity could be embarrassing because we were critiqued by management and our peers. It soon became a competition among the sales team managers—who could throw the biggest curve ball to the other "role player" to show how much more you knew? The exercise did model ways to present new product information, and in its own way built our confidence by giving us an opportunity to practice.

This time around, analyzing my peers, I realized we were all type-A perfectionists. We had a knack for looking calm and professional while on the inside we were screaming to get out of this chokehold of a job where, I swear, I saw the words "Welcome To Your Stressed-Out Life" each day I opened the office door. As you'd expect, the environment at this company did nothing to keep managers in their jobs—there was a high burnout rate.

There were new problems I had to face with confidence and flexibility with the new sales position. Day-to-day challenges continued, like a client questioning charges on their bill or whether a mouse may have eaten a granola bar right off their desk (an unusual case but it happened). And I was starting from scratch, managing a location that wasn't working from the front desk to the automatic locks on the doors.

I remember the day, exactly six months after I had taken on the new office burden. While sitting in traffic on the exit ramp marked "Stress Boulevard," running late for my next appointment, I decided my six months at the new location were up.

What would they do if I put in two weeks' notice? Would they be mad I didn't give them enough time to find a replacement? I felt guilty, like I owed them more, and I wanted to be nice, so I gave them three weeks. I didn't want anyone to be inconvenienced because I was leaving. (Would a man think this way? Or was this a female guilt thing I was experiencing? Was this a sign of weakness? Stress made me question every step of the decision.)

I had trained new managers and knew how much time they needed to be indoctrinated, so I felt giving my boss more time to find a replacement was the right thing to do. And of course, they would hate to lose such a hard worker like me.

But I found it wasn't like that at all. They didn't rush to hire anyone. They just dumped my responsibilities onto another overstressed manager. Déjà vu all over again. I became another one of their burned-out, unappreciated employees who were easily replaced. I knew at that point: I had made the right decision to move on.

In retrospect, though, what the heck was I thinking when I *took* the job? I already knew that successful sales work led to more work responsibility at the best of companies. I had read about this company online and found stories about their treatment of employees before I signed a contract. I saw the writing on the wall before I even started, but I didn't pay attention to the red flags about the toxic culture.

You can't change management, especially if it's bad management. None of this was my fault; I just chose a place to work that had a questionable reputation for how employees are treated. And they treated me exactly as the other employee complaints predicted.

It's important to find a company culture that respects employees, and where your sales successes lead to more work *you* want to do. Because wherever you work, you'll hear, "Good job! Now sell more!" Your confidence will help you make the right choices and negotiate promotions that will feel like an adventure, not a burden.

Even at a well-respected business, there are still challenges the sales team faces. In the case of my TV station selling experience, cameras were commonly used not just for on-air talent, but for sales team training. I thought we had a strong team that brought in a lot of business, but management wanted to be sure we were saying everything right to win more deals.

We were *filmed* in a high-stakes role-playing exercise—never a crowd favorite. We each made a sales presentation to managers and then had to react while on camera to whatever they threw at us. The manager who acted as my prospect interrupted my presentation by leaving the room with the camera continuing to record my reaction—which was disbelief that he would be so rude. I guess he thought a client might do this. Maybe to him but never to me. Turns out, this did happen a few months later. The same manager hijacked *my* presentation to a real prospect, who walked out, resulting in a lost deal.

Then we watched the recordings back as a group and critiqued them. In theory, we were meant to view our peers more critically and help them improve. In practice, we felt embarrassed in front of everyone else. I remember after this exercise it wasn't long until the weaker salespeople were gone. Those of us with the confidence to persevere stayed despite the experience.

Training and recognition are handled differently depending on a business's culture. I must say, the TV station did reward us with a special celebration for a job well done when we exceeded sales in each quarter. When I worked for Pampered Chef, I was able to reach sales goals after a few years of trying, which allowed me to enjoy a free vacation with my family. At the computer manufacturer, our sales team's successes were recognized regularly by our general manager with various incentives like a day off and special luncheons that kept us on track and productive. And I remember how appreciated I felt when I opened the signature blue box from Tiffany with a small mantel clock as a thank you for my hard work as a top performer on the sales team.

Would I have still worked that hard knowing I was going to get rewarded? Yes, I had my own personal work ethic and goals to reach, no matter what the reward. But I was happier at the firms with healthier company cultures. Getting rewards helped our teams build loyalty and connections; getting punished with overwork caused only burnout.

I may have been spoiled by the computer company when I received that expensive gift. At another job I got a turkey like everyone else for Thanksgiving. But I liked sales work, and I didn't even expect the turkey. I came to appreciate that regular thank-you token as a sign I was in the right place—every blessed year.

Sales are about making money and the organization's success depends on that. It comes down to what you're willing to tolerate on the road to that success—and whether you're willing to work with good or bad management, or only with a company culture and product that fits your sales style and values.

In sales, success is never enough, and it's measured differently by each employer. You must jump higher by adjusting the bar to reach those goals and constantly work at making improvements, internal and external pressures you have to balance yourself.

Dealing with all those pressures does build confidence over time. Maybe if I wasn't such a perfectionist, I would have had less stress in my life. I had to learn to manage my stress, because if you're not healthy, you can't do your job very well. I just had to learn the hard way.

Anyone in a sales career who is doing it just for recognition will be continually disappointed. It's better not to have those expectations and then be surprised by getting more back for what you do, even if it is a free Thanksgiving turkey.

9

TURNING LEMONS
INTO LEMON DROP MARTINIS

———•———

F orget the lemonade. I prefer lemon drop martinis. What better reward is there when life gives you lemons? Sweet and sour with a little kick. A celebratory beverage for reaching or exceeding a goal or overcoming an obstacle.

Martinis are also perfect for celebrating friendships. I have a circle of "Tini" girlfriends. Throughout our times together we would drink to life's little celebrations and support each other through challenges. We even had our own martini nicknames etched onto our personal glasses—Jeantini, Nancytini, etc. It was almost like raising a toast with the "I'm Thumbody!" mug but with vodka.

Life's personal and professional crises can happen when you least expect them. The first lemon for me was a cancer diagnosis. After I quit selling office space, I had only been in my next, less stressful job for three months. I was selling magazine ads when I was told I needed to have surgery and start chemo treatment.

That was a lot of lemons to deal with. I had to decide how I wanted to make the best of the situation—managing a timeline to get through this with the promise of a martini waiting for me at the end of the chemo tunnel.

I decided, after talking it over with my understanding boss at the magazine, to continue working through treatment even though it would be tough. I remember standing at the base of the stairs that led to our third-floor office loft. I had been in treatment for a few months and was really weak, but I had to show that I was up to the challenge.

It became the most tiring flight of stairs I had ever climbed. I felt victorious just making it to the top. I remember after completing that last step to get there and a little out of breath, my coworker saw me and looked concerned.

She had experienced the big C herself years before. She asked what I was doing there and that maybe I should be home, in bed. I wished she had been more supportive of my decision to be at work. But I guess telling me to go home was instead her way of showing support, and I must have looked as exhausted as I felt. I appreciated the concern, but ultimately, it was my bowl of lemons, and I could make whatever I wanted out of them—that martini was waiting.

As a contractor at the magazine, I didn't have the pressure of a corporate position and I was able to set my own hours. I could make appointments around treatments and have as much of a normal life as possible. I found that having a positive attitude and an understanding boss made a huge difference in successfully beating the disease and continuing my success in sales. Even meeting with clients, if I was not feeling up to a face-to-face call, I could reschedule. But sometimes I pushed myself. It helped me stay confident in my recovery, and my work.

I was trying to get an appointment with the manager of the Silver Diner restaurant. I had called for weeks to get him to agree to meet. Unfortunately, the date we scheduled was my chemo day. I felt crappy, but I knew I could not put off this opportunity any longer.

I asked my husband to come with me for moral support or to pick me up off the floor if necessary. I didn't tell the prospect I was on chemo, but what I didn't realize was that I looked like I was. I was pale, had lost all my hair, and wore a wig. I had to draw on my eyebrows, and I had no eyelashes. I kept thinking, if he only knew what it took for me to gather the energy to get through this meeting. I didn't want to seem weak. I thought I had to just fake it.

He offered me lunch and I turned it down, even though I adored their food. I really wanted a milkshake but the thought of it made me sick. Our meeting went well, and it was the first step to winning their business. Later, I told him I was in treatment, and that's why I couldn't eat the food he knew I loved. I was tired of being strong.

To this day, that manager still greets me with a hug and asks how I am doing. I decided after that experience it was okay to let someone know what I was going through. It was better to be honest and take care of myself, hoping that someone would feel a little empathy toward me. More often than not, they did. That little triumph was part of my martini celebration a few months later.

Despite my health setback, in my first eighteen months at the magazine I brought in sixty new clients. I loved it for three years until I started getting hungrier for more challenges. A sales manager I knew at a local television station pursued me to work for him. Feeling better physically and ready to start a new chapter, I accepted the new job.

It was 2019 and the world was my oyster at that point. I had a reputation for my sales work and went on to bring in the clients the sales manager was eager to get. I was networking, selling to new prospects, and had contracts and leads in the pipeline. Soon, I had a year under my belt, and I felt confident that I had earned those lemon drop martinis.

Then it happened, the external crisis no one could have predicted, COVID-19 in March 2020, and the world shut down. Throw out the networking, selling to people in person, and closing those waiting deals. There was so much uncertainty, budgets were being cut and advertising was the first to go. All I could think was, please don't let me lose a big account.

Then I got the call. It was the legendary car dealership's ad agency. I had worked so hard to get this client and they just started their campaign. With such uncertainty in the market, they stopped running their commercials. No one was buying cars. How could a salesperson survive this?

My sales manager was scrambling to find a way for our team to move forward and bring in new business. We had to ask tough questions. What businesses were in demand during this time? Who was making money? Who was not making money? How do we make a presentation if we can't be there in person?

The challenge during this crisis was how to regroup and remain a successful selling team. We were being pelted by lemons and it was time to make something out of them (a martini was sounding really great about then)—with ingredients that included new sales strategies.

PANDEMIC PANIC SOLUTION #1

Dialing for dollars.

I always thought my greatest strengths were networking and selling in person. I loved the social aspect of my job. I now needed to make that personal connection and sharpen my communication skills in other ways. Time to get serious and make cold-calling on the phone a priority, using that personal charm I was so lucky to have. This is where the confidence had to kick in.

How can I empathize with the prospect about the pandemic predicament and help their business? We had "phone-a-thons" where the sales team would put a couple hours aside a day to "dial for dollars." It was a much more positive experience than a "war room" scenario for focusing on getting more business.

I developed better relationships with prospects and clients. We were all in the same lifeboat—facing the uncertainties of the current times and riding the waves. I had heart-to-heart talks with management at nursing homes who were my clients and now dealing with lockdowns at their facilities. They couldn't take new patients and were losing employees. We had to change their ad strategy to fit the moment; show their compassionate side while asking for new care-givers to apply. We had to accept that the process of seeing results could take more time than usual.

PANDEMIC PANIC SOLUTION #2

Make a sales pitch in a box.

Since we couldn't be in face-to-face meetings, a virtual Zoom meeting was the only way to do business. Emailing a presentation just didn't cut it, so we met virtually. It was like selling in a box. Seeing the prospect and using the computer screen to make our pitches really helped with sales. In fact, I had thought it would be more difficult to get to *yes* without being there in the same room, but I was wrong. I had some well-tailored presentations that provided the solutions they needed to make decisions on the spot.

I was having more Zoom meetings in a day than I would have otherwise had face-to-face meetings that I would be traveling to. Using virtual technology in a time when there were not many choices was a lifesaver. Learning how to use it effectively was also a challenge.

I always had my lipstick beside my computer for a quick pick-me-up before I started the meeting and improved the background by putting a bouquet of flowers behind me for my client's viewing pleasure. Whatever it took to make the meeting in the box more inviting to get the sale—and it worked. People noticed and complimented me on how I looked and the flowers in the room. It was comforting to connect with *someone* despite the distance.

PANDEMIC PANIC SOLUTION #3

Take advantage of changes in the market.

Not every business makes money during times of crisis. I was ready to close a deal before the pandemic with a theater company when entertainment venues closed. But grocery stores and home improvement companies were doing well during the shutdown while people were staying at home. That's when I was finally able to secure the grocery store prospect my manager had lost months before.

Successful marketers adapt to current circumstances. It was easier to pivot and see the opportunities in front of us instead of complaining about lost business. Never did I think how flexible I would have to be in my sales techniques and attitude to make my sales goals. But I had developed my confidence through a long track record, and as I identified new markets, I found a way to turn connections into contracts.

I was having conversations with business owners and empathizing with their plights of needing to get more employees. There were those lemons. I helped them with solutions to advertise for employment, which had never been a big sector of our business.

On the other side, a hobby store owner was doing more business than ever because people had more leisure time on their hands. He had money to spend on more advertising, and I was happy to help him use it. I was starting to make martinis again.

PANDEMIC PANIC SOLUTION #4

Don't forget the clients who helped you through the tough times.

I remember my boss at the magazine telling me that if it weren't for his loyal clients, he would have never made it through the last recession. When you are good to your clients, they will be good to you. Tell them how much their business means to you, especially when times are tough. If you must provide special pricing for them to afford your services, then do what is mutually beneficial to keep that long-term relationship.

There *will* be an end to the crisis, and we will raise that martini glass together. I had many clients thank me for working with them on their campaigns so we could continue doing business together. That customer service will long be remembered. It turned into both of us being "Thumbody" to each other.

We can't always control an internal or external crisis from happening; we just find ways to deal with it. Sometimes when you expect support, especially from someone on a personal level, you must instead find that strength within yourself to move forward.

I expected my peers to be supportive of my health choices, but I had to find my own strength to deal with the lemons that came my way. It was my internal struggle and I had to summon the positivity within me to get my own personal win. It was as if climbing those stairs to have my victory dance at the top each day kept the celebration of a lemon martini within my reach.

The pandemic was an equally challenging external crisis. A team approach with the sales managers helped us transform all the lemons being thrown at us—rediscovering and developing tools to combat the crisis so we could find internal strength to become successful and celebrate together.

In the end, the (lemon drop martini) recipe for success is simple—squeeze everything out of the lemons, add a sweet ingredient of positivity for balance, follow by shaking things up a bit for proper mixing, then strain out the negativity and pour the rest into the glass for a perfect result—a win, a new client, a happy client, and a successful salesperson—despite it all.

10

TO BE OR NOT TO BE A CONFIDENT SALESPERSON

———·———

Ask any actor how they feel each time they go on stage, and some may tell you they are nervous wrecks. How can that be? They're professionals who have perfected their craft. They look so confident.

I was an actor in high school theater and enjoyed being on the stage, but I was scared to death that I would forget my lines. It was well into my adult life that I would still have nightmares about it. I hadn't acted since my late teens and the fear was still embedded in my psyche.

I guess everyone has stage fright. Whether it's standing under the spotlight and delivering lines to a captive audience or sitting in front of the prospect whose eyes are laser-focused on you while you're making the sales pitch—it's really the same thing.

I'd like to admit right now that being in sales made me nervous, too, especially at the beginning of my career. You would never know from my outward appearance since I always looked confident. I had to prospect for new business constantly, face strangers and tell them why parting with their money was a good idea, and then have the guts to make them trust me and sign on the dotted line. Who would do this every day?

But wait. I believe selling something to someone makes them feel excited and loved. Just like actors, there's nothing like seeing their names in lights. When I sold TV commercials and magazine ads, the client was so excited to appear in their own commercial or in the colorful magazine ad. It was glamorous. Their business became famous, and the product really sold itself.

All I had to do was help them get what they wanted and put them out there as the expert for the world to see. As a campaign progresses and is successful, they continue to do business with me. Making someone feel special or loved is something we can control as sales professionals, and it sells anything better than any scientific sales formula.

I've always been the person who wants to be in control. Let's face it—many women are like that. We learn to be good at lovingly controlling our spouse, children, friends, and family members. Why not use our natural gifts?

We use sales techniques to persuade members of our household to do a task, and then they get something in return—tell the children to get their homework done and they get ice cream, get the husband to fix the leaky faucet and he'll get, well, something nice.

So, why shouldn't being a salesperson be easy for a woman? Yet most women don't embrace sales as something they think they can do, let alone like. If they can just feel confident about building relationships they can control in a sales situation, they're almost there.

When the women at PC shows said to me, "I could never do what you do," I would realize that I look successful to others—I ask for the sale, I get the sale (usually), and I am perceived as the expert. And more importantly, I show confidence. But it always made me a little sad to see the way they underestimated themselves.

I believe that if some women had more confidence in how they present themselves then they would be more confident selling. They may not realize how much they already believe in the product. If they could just get past the word "salesperson" that in itself would be a confidence booster.

A member of my women's business group told me she likes to sell but she's afraid to close. This surprised me because I knew she loved the skin-care products she sold, and I assumed she was an excellent salesperson.

But I'll never forget that "help me" look in her eyes when she asked me what the secret was to closing a deal. She didn't feel comfortable asking for the business, she said. I had to point out her apparent confidence and enthusiasm she had for the products.

I told her to try the "I love it and you'll love it too" close. She looked at me with a surprised expression and said she never thought of it that way. She was thinking of some formulaic closing script instead of just being herself and showing her absolute trust and confidence in the product, thus encouraging the prospect to buy.

Perhaps it was this intense belief in my products that helped me be so successful in my sales career. Without sales experience, I was able to have the confidence to learn and succeed. When I sold Girl Scout Cookies, I didn't know about rejection, yet I was excited to ask someone to buy something I liked. If they said *no*, I wouldn't give up; I just moved on to the next house. I knew how much I loved the product and kept hoping they would too. So, with persistence, I gained more self-confidence selling, which turned into more sales, which turned into greater confidence that whatever adventure came my way, I was up for it.

In the same way, when I sold kitchen tools, it was mostly the joy of presenting something I loved to the audience of homemakers. Was it also strategic? Of course. I did want them to buy one of the expensive stoneware items so I could make the commission I needed to contribute to the mortgage each month. If they were happy with their purchase so their kids could have the best-tasting pizza ever, so was I, but for different reasons.

I never think of myself as someone who knows everything about sales. If that were the case, I would be the most successful salesperson of all time. For most of my career, I had to sell enough to make a quota or reach a specific goal set by management, all the while trying to make each client happy. And then every sales job was different with goals that didn't necessarily put client happiness first. I did well because I believed in myself and kept working toward my goals.

There were times I've had to "fake it to make it." Like being hired for a management position when I had never had that experience. I was hired for that position because I showed confidence in my abilities and the potential to be a great contributor to the organization.

No one (except perhaps your boss) knows if you are really the best at what you do. If the illusion is there, use it. You can catch up and learn what you need to while you're working it. Some jobs require you to know a lot in a short period of time. As a former boss told me, "Get ready, there's so much information coming at you; it's like being pelted by a powerful fire hose."

It can feel that way with onboarding and training. It's a long process with tons of information coming your way at warp speed. Then, before you think you're ready, they throw you to the sharks and you either sink or swim. I learned to keep swimming while taking lessons, so that I would be further ahead of the others when I touched the wall. After gulping a lot of water in one training period, I remember saying to myself, "I finally get it." All the pieces of the job just gelled, and the selling process came that much easier.

Sometimes you can get a taste of the martini early, especially when things are going well. You are swimming so hard; you don't realize how successful you've already become. When I was selling offices, I was told by management I was one of the top performers in the company. Then, I was whisked away to a meeting at corporate with my high-achieving peers.

They told us we were "the cream of the crop," which I assume was supposed to make us feel appreciated, but those were code words for "continue being superhumans." It was nice to be recognized but I had to learn to get some human balance, so I could keep swimming. I started recognizing the hard-driving culture of that company when the female facilitator of a training class said confidently that during a surgical procedure, she had her cell phone in her hand because she was *that* important.

I was faced with a choice: to be or not to be like that person. If that was the prevailing train of thought in the organization, I did *not* ever want to be her. Whenever I felt I was out of balance, I had to stop and ask myself how far I would go as that Type-A person and whether it was worth it. I don't know if women think that way enough. We're told to keep reaching for that gold ring, no matter how much it takes out of us. We try to be superhuman in everything we do, showing strength and being successful in every way. That's just not sustainable.

But ambition and confidence are important, because they keep us going, and lead to great sales success as well as life satisfaction. Curiously, the "women can do it all" mentality was quite prevalent throughout my career—whether single or married. Was I going to go for it all or think about doing what was best for me in whatever stage I was in?

In my early career days, a high-achieving girlfriend often said we were "Women of the '80s," whatever that meant in the decade of greed, material girls, and climbing the corporate ladder. As women we didn't realize how hard we were working to prove ourselves. I could compete with men in the same positions at most of my jobs and be included in the "cream of the crop" group like they were.

And then there were the dating experiences when I was told once by a boyfriend that I would always be more successful in my career than he would ever be. And told by another that he couldn't believe I made more money than he did. Neither of them ever proposed.

I had an eight-year career after college before I got married. My husband, Tom, was different from the insecure men I had dated. He was confident and made me feel respected. I was able to work part-time and then full-time when my children were growing up. I learned a little balance and gained a lot of confidence.

Thankfully, we've finally started admitting that having it all isn't quite what it's cracked up to be. Burnout and health problems can rear their ugly heads. Fortunately, now there's more emphasis on wellness and making choices where we want to really excel in our lives. Realizing "I am enough" fuels confidence, helping us feel good about what we've accomplished.

If I've gained anything through my sales career experience, it's not only the satisfaction I found in my ability to succeed but assurance that what I've done has been right for me—taking care of my health, having time for family, and having no regrets about the amazing career path I took.

11

THE CLOSE

W hen I first entered the business world, all I wanted was to be a good, dependable worker. The six attributes that were my foundation for building confidence were: hard work, speaking skills, appearance, character, honesty, and dependability. These were my values, and I wanted to be a person who embodied them. It turned out these characteristics brought me success for years in all my sales jobs.

I learned these values from my family. My father had his own business, and my mother was his bookkeeper. She showed me her strong side in dealing with customers. At times she had to gather her confidence and knock on a customer's door, politely asking them to pay their past-due bills. That took guts. It was what she had to do to keep the business afloat. Sometimes I did the same thing in my sales jobs—confidently asking the client whose account was overdue to please pay their bill or I don't get paid.

My mother also taught me the importance of speaking and writing skills as well as appearance and presenting myself, help-ing me with wardrobe choices for interviews in those early days, encouraging me to talk on the phone and represent myself confidently, and providing grammatical advice for writing.

When I started writing this book, I felt my success was worth talking about, especially since I had positive reinforcement from other women I knew in sales. I saw how so many women underestimated their gifts, downplaying or sabotaging their success in sales. I began sharing my stories and mentoring women who were experiencing similar feelings about their confidence levels and how they were viewed as salespeople. They learned they were not alone and what I had to share could help.

For women in sales, selling confidence doesn't mean being an aggressive used-car salesman. Confidence is built by being your authentic self—showing genuineness in your presentation and using persistence and patience during the sales process—then proving to each client that you're trustworthy, honest, and dependable, which builds a strong business relationship. Aggressive behavior is nowhere to be found in these techniques.

Then there's the support you get from others who are important to you. I had a rocky start with parents who didn't understand my desire to sell cookies. But with the confidence I built when I persuaded them I could do it, and then with my sales, I turned that discouragement into happy customers—proving to mom and dad that I could be successful. That's when I won their support and encouragement.

Before I signed up to sell Pampered Chef products, I had the support of my incredibly understanding husband. Fortunately, I already had a successful sales track record to build my case. He saw the desire in me to sell and the potential for contributing to the family income.

As life changed, my husband was very encouraging as my career took lots of turns, from my California move years ago, to supporting my decision to work while in cancer treatment. He knew that my experiences would make me stronger and that I could show others, especially women, how to make it if they were in the same situation.

Sometimes you must find the best way to handle life's challenges—in my case, coming of age and dealing with challenges brought on by a reawakening of women's roles in the workforce and finding strength during tough times. These learning experiences gave me confidence and a strong foundation for being a successful saleswoman, mother, wife, and community member.

In my career, every step I took on the job ladder—even the red-flag experiences—was a step up to a higher challenge. The confidence I gained made me a stronger candidate for the next job. I achieved a reputation for being a professional salesperson who was respected by managers, business owners, clients, and my peers. I created my own selling style while striving to be an expert in my field. I was persistent without ever needing to be overly aggressive.

I never modeled myself after someone whose style I didn't like, but after those who were successful, and who I could respect. I took cues from them by dressing professionally (which sometimes included wearing power heels) and preparing myself mentally before walking into a roomful of strangers. It really helped me to be more aware of the whole package of self-presentation, so I could feel in control and confident handling any situation.

Everyone who has a product or service to sell is capable of being a confident salesperson. Young or old, male or female—there are lessons to be learned from experiences that build confidence—like navigating through the quagmire of self-doubt and then realizing that your style of selling is unique, and that it works for you.

Dealing with uncomfortable situations like addressing a prospect's concerns and helping them feel confident about working with you will be worth the effort when they become your client.

So, what's the takeaway? What it all comes down to is confidence with sales is twofold—selling *confidence* and *selling* confidence.

You *are* that confident person with the knowledge and character attributes who is perceived as a unique package. There is no one like you with the style, presence, knowledge, or honesty you have, just you and your unique power to win people over. Negative stereotypes fade away when you create strong sales relationships.

You are also that *selling* machine with skills and expertise that you show during the sales process. You believe in what you're selling, you have the talent to overcome obstacles, and you know how to persuade them to say *yes*—confidently. Gaining experience by selling different products, learning sales techniques, and applying them to all situations builds that confidence.

Combining these two aspects of personal and professional confidence will help you and your career be more successful. Staying the course, building a reputation, continually educating yourself, and knowing there is a martini on the horizon for every challenge out there makes that *win* one to savor and enjoy.

APPENDIX

ABOUT THE AUTHOR

Jean Wright wants women to know they have the potential to excel in the world of sales. Her career spans four decades of selling experience with corporations, nonprofits, and media companies. Her roots are in Pittsburgh, where her father ran a painting company he built as an immigrant and her mother supported him with her business skills. Jean credits her parents' example of how to run a successful business for her strong work ethic and confident attitude.

A graduate of Marywood University with a BA in Communication Arts, with a concentration in Radio and TV, Jean found creative ways to effectively use her skills for public speaking and writing. She had early success working in Washington, DC, and Los Angeles for the National Captioning Institute marketing to clients in the television industry. She also worked in sales for personnel agencies, sports entertainment, business office services, and organizations, as well as print and digital media companies. She has been recognized for excellence in customer service and sales as well as being promoted to sales management–level positions.

Jean's aha moment came as the president of a women's business organization where she met sales entrepreneurs experiencing confidence problems. The desire to help women raise their confidence levels in sales motivated her to write her first book, *Selling Your Confidence: Forging a Successful Sales Career from Mint Cookies to Martinis*. Her career journey takes the reader on a path strewn with confidence-building challenges that many women may encounter during their own careers. Jean speaks to business organizations and women's groups about confidence-building and has her own consulting practice to help entrepreneurs and sales teams.

Frederick, Maryland, has been her adopted home for thirty years. She and her husband, Tom, have two grown children and enjoy small-town life. They especially enjoy the rich history and charm of the greater Washington, DC region for short getaway trips, and the best in entertainment venues.

Connect with Jean on social media:

https://www.linkedin.com/in/jeanwright-confidencebuilder/
https://www.facebook.com/groups/sellingyourconfidence
https://www.instagram.com/jeanw9440/

Sales Confidence Expert

Build Relationships
Sell Authentically
Close Confidently

Take your confidence to a higher level

Jean Wright, Sales Confidence Builder, Sales Coach and Professional Speaker is the author of *Selling Your Confidence.*

Sales Team Coaching

Speaker & Presenter

Understanding Your Sales Potential

For a complimentary consultation visit
www.sellingyourconfidence.com

Made in the USA
Middletown, DE
07 June 2023